TODAY'S MEDIEVAL UNIVERSITY

PAST IMPERFECT

Past Imperfect presents concise critical overviews of the latest research by the world's leading scholars. Subjects cross the full range of fields in the period ca. 400—1500 CE which, in a European context, is known as the Middle Ages. Anyone interested in this period will be enthralled and enlightened by these overviews, written in provocative but accessible language. These affordable paperbacks prove that the era still retains a powerful resonance and impact throughout the world today.

Director and Editor-in-Chief

Simon Forde, *Western Michigan University*

Acquisitions Editors

Shannon Cunningham, *Milwaukee*
Ruth Kennedy, *Adelaide*

Production

Linda K. Judy, *Kalamazoo*

TODAY'S MEDIEVAL UNIVERSITY

M. J. Toswell

Library of Congress Cataloging in Publication Data

Names: Toswell, M. J.
Title: Today's medieval university / M. J. Toswell.
Description: Kalamazoo : Medieval Institute Publications, Western Michigan
    University, [2016] | Series: Past imperfect series | Includes
    bibliographical references.
Identifiers: LCCN 2016043796 (print) | LCCN 2016051726 (ebook) | ISBN
    9781942401179 (paperbound : alk. paper) | ISBN 9781942401186
Subjects: LCSH: Education, Higher--Philosophy. | Medievalism.
Classification: LCC LB2322.2 .T59 2016 (print) | LCC LB2322.2 (ebook) | DDC
    378.001--dc23
LC record available at https://lccn.loc.gov/2016043796

ISBN 978-1-942401-17-9
e-ISBN 978-1-942401-18-6

mip-archumanitiespress.org

Printed and bound by CPI Group (UK) Ltd, Croydon

To the Academic Senate of the University of Western Ontario. This book is dedicated to the thoughtful and intelligent colleagues (on all sides of the issues) who demonstrated, in spring 2015, that good governance and academic integrity are the muscles of the university. Muscles atrophy when insufficiently used. We used ours correctly. The real issue is whether we will continue so to do.

Contents

Preface

I want to thank Erin T. Dailey for pushing me enthusiastically to write this piece back when it was a slightly odd thought at Leeds 2015, and Simon Forde, Ruth Kennedy, and Shannon Cunningham for curating its arrival to the press, and progress through publication. Angela Weisl considerably sharpened the focus, especially of the second and third chapters, and I am grateful for her perspicacious eye and gracious review. Some of the material here first saw the light of critical engagement at the October 2015 conference in Pittsburgh of the ISSM (International Society for Studies in Medievalism), and I am also grateful for encouragement offered there.

University governance has been a special field of study for me, mostly as a *practicum*, for over thirty years. I'm going to skip past all the details, because they're more than a bit depressing, but, yes, I'm a university governance junkie. I have discussed university governance issues with uncounted numbers of colleagues both at Western and at many other universities, at conferences and at coffeehouses, on buses and on trains, and I'm a real menace at dinner parties and formal hall meals. I am very grateful to all those who have talked with me, argued with me, debated with me, and shouted at me in various institutional locations—I will leave you all blessedly anonymous. I will take full credit for all the

errors and misconceptions, as well as the occasional seren-
dipitous thought, in the following.

Given the parameters of this series, and in order to make
my argument as clear as possible, I have used the terminol-
ogy of the medieval university only where it is genuinely
necessary, and I have either translated myself or made use
of available translations for statutes, regulations, and scholarship not in English. This has been handy in many ways,
as the principal texts about how the medieval university
worked were written in an age in which footnotes could be
very brief, and quite aggravating, and in fact the best stories
have no references at all. I've had to give up on some good
anecdotes that I could not verify (the supposed medieval
endowment to give Merton College a continental chef comes
briefly to mind), but I hope I've kept enough detail to help
with the argument.

September 29, 2016

Introduction

Given the complexities of the interlocking pieces, universities function surprisingly well. Professors teach and accomplish their research, and some of them engage in devoted service to the institution, to their own field, or even to the academy more generally. Students learn and grow up, and begin to engage with the world as independent operators. Some of them choose to go on to graduate schools, including more detailed studies in a discipline or professional schools of various kinds. They complete their programs of study successfully and they advance to their futures with baccalaureates, master's degrees, and doctorates. Staff members and administrators successfully organize degrees, reports, materials, and faculties; other staff members and administrators face up to problems of parking, buildings, grounds, housing, food, transport, and that great bugbear of universities: deferred maintenance. Senior administrators face outwards to governments and donors, and inwards to coordinate and set policy and direction for the university entrusted to their care. Alumni engage in various kinds of intervention and work. Mostly, they find themselves appreciated for their donations and naming opportunities, and mostly underappreciated for their willingness to intervene in current events with remembrances and reminiscences.

They also return to their *alma mater* for major events and celebrations. Research happens. Teaching happens.

While universities are seldom well-oiled machines, they get the job done. In fact, many would argue, and have argued, that the crankiness inherent in the university system is perhaps its greatest strength. Courses can, in the hands of different faculty members, offer quite extraordinarily different experiences for those taking them and those offering them: one might be a highly interactive and tense experience in the classroom, with questions zinging and responses queried; another might offer podcasts of the lectures with a flipped classroom investigating details or solving problems; and another might split the class up into groups investigating a given problem not just in the classroom but for its application in the community, or indeed in a different community or country. Each of these learning experiences is equally valid, will appeal more to some students than others, and will challenge some students to a greater degree than others. Each experience offers some utility, some knowledge, some opportunity for growth and development to the individual student and to the community. The great strength of a university is that it can encompass them all, and faculty members who engage properly with their academic responsibilities will pursue what they see as the best approach. A similar ethos ought, of course, to apply to the research accomplished in a university by the many layers of individuals involved, from technicians to graduate and undergraduate interns and work-experience contributors, to post-graduate and post-doctoral researchers, to faculty members and team leaders. The single individual working alone in an office trying to think new thoughts should have the time and space necessary for that work, as should the heavy-hitting scientist leading three major research teams and managing a multi-million-dollar budget, as should the health sciences researcher managing projects in the community, the hospital, and in another country with partnership grants and private-sector support. That is, the sheer range and scope of approaches at a university demonstrate the inherent elasticity, the flexibility of the university construct. A small liberal-arts college or a university located in a distant region of the country offers essentially the same structure and approach as the large metropolitan university, the high-end privately endowed collegiate university, or the state-founded and state-funded educational institution established where there is tremendous room to grow in its own vast donated lands. Every institution offers a disparate collection of ways to learn, to teach, and to research, and the majority of those institutions are governed by a mixture of faculty, administrators, volunteers from the community and the alumni, and the students (often nowadays called the clients or even the stake-holders, a term that lumps them together with every other worker on the campus who is not a senior administrator). Somehow, this unexpected mix of actors and re-actors, professors and students, individuals and groups, young and old, scientists and artsies, men and women get the job done. Bluntly put, universities function.

Individual universities perforce have exceptionalist tendencies. They draw attention to fine differences in the behaviour patterns, niche programmes that are hallmarks of the individual institution, governance structures, culture, quality of the student body, excellence and engagement of the faculty. Some have local traditions and celebrations by which they set inordinate store, and by which they identify themselves as unique and special. Every university, whether it wishes to or not, has a brand, a public image that changes little but that marks its perception for its graduates, its potential students, and the general public. Universities foster and develop their brand equity, since the public perception of a university is enduring, inelastic, and usually slow to change. In itself, that public perception of the enduring use of a university is often the single greatest asset of the system of universities in most countries. If university budgets included a reporting line for goodwill, it would in most cases be an enormous, off-the-charts asset. Even the smallest liberal college in a small town generates goodwill and brand equity far beyond what its relative size would suggest. The general public is proud of its universities, and thinks of them with a kind of fond pride. Of course, this general sense of approbation also carries with it a willingness to blame individual universities, sometimes in quite shocking terms, for their political correctness, their financial irresponsibility, their pointless research, or their leftwing tendencies as foisted holus-bolus upon their students. Somehow, however, these attacks on universities do not contribute to any generalized diminution in the reverence and pleasure taken in the idea of having a local university. Universities are a public good, as recognized by the public.

The differences among universities are as a rule surprisingly minor. The basic structure of a university is surprisingly robust. Further, a very great strength of the collegiate decision-making of a university is its well-known slowness to change. A joke often told, with rueful pride, in the university system is that an innovation adopted in the business sector in a couple of months and the government sector in a year or eighteen months will take several years to wend its way through the roadblocks and systems of a given university, let alone the whole university sector. Universities are ponderous entities, not prone to rapid change or instant decision-making. My project here is to consider some of the parameters of that imperviousness, that rather monolithic lack of nimble dance moves in the pavane that is the post-secondary education sector as originated in western Europe, exported to North America and Australasia, and more recently to the globe. The focus will be something of a fuzzy set, universities from medieval Europe or founded along similar lines. At some points in my argument, the fuzzy set will include virtually all the universities with this Western-inflected structure, and at others the set may identify a somewhat narrower group. At the outset it seems best to take a broad view, and let the more specific ones develop as they must.

This fuzzy set does, however, begin with the foundation of the European universities at the end of the eleventh century or the beginning of the twelfth century in Bologna, Salerno, Paris, Oxford, and shortly thereafter in many locations in the rest of Europe. A development from the cathedral schools and the monasteries, the first universities were closely tied both to the hierarchy of the Christian church and to the monarchies and empires of the day. Their structures, their set texts, their rituals: all these elements were established in one university and replicated in all the others so rapidly that in most cases the origin of a given element can only rarely be traced. At the turn of the thirteenth century the main elements of the medieval university were already in place, and by the turn of the fourteenth century the pattern of the Western university was largely set. It began with the *studium generale*, the set curriculum intended for senior scholars, but which came to refer to the entity which is a *universitas*, a guild of the whole, those who are engaged in teaching and studying the *studium generale*. Students arrived young, already trained in the *trivium* (grammar, rhetoric, logic) and the *quadrivium* (arithmetic, geometry, music, astronomy), generally to towns or cities, and took up their advanced studies with a master directly, and more indirectly in paid lectures with other masters. Initially a group of students would align with a particular regent master in a college, while subscribing also to the *universitas* and its structure of examinations, organized lectures, and discipline. Buildings came later, and unsurprisingly they reflected the ecclesiastical patterning behind much of the early university system.

The architecture of masters and students living close to one another was directly comparable to the architecture in a monastery or nunnery with avowed monastics and oblates. By the end of the fourteenth century, the monastic architecture of the nascent university had altered into the college cloister and the university lecture hall and administrative offices, sometimes overlapping with each other and sometimes not. This was never a comfortable and easy development, however, and it was heavily influenced by local conditions of culture, economy, and governance. Universities were greatly desired by many cities and towns, and were seen as a benefit to the local economy and to local prestige. They were meeting places for scholars, nexus points where the municipal, ecclesiastical, and noble or royal desires all intersected to create cooperative new endeavours.

After the initial establishment of a *universitas*, however, great variations in development occurred. Some withered and collapsed or nearly collapsed under the weight of funding problems or town and gown conflicts; others developed specialist faculties rather than the *studium generale*; some flourished with excellent teachers and students; some had trouble acquiring funds to establish buildings and develop the treasuries needed to fund their expansion or indeed their existence. Funding and ethos were always already in crisis. Problems and challenges of this sort are still around today. As Jaroslav Pelikan, the eminent public intellectual and medievalist writes in his study of the idea of the university, revivifying and reconsidering John Henry Newman's famous attempt at defining the role of the university in the nineteenth century, "A modern society is unthinkable without the university," but a few lines later "the university is in a state of crisis and is in danger of losing credibility."[1] In other words, the university is a fixture in Western society, but a fixture that requires extensive renovation. At the same time, in Pelikan's view, that renovation must maintain a sense of the history of the institution, taking what is of value from that tradition, and must always look back before rushing forward into the twenty-first century. The university, or the *universitas*, was wholly an invention of the European Middle Ages; it has no precedents in antiquity, in the Graeco-Roman tradition, nor any clear parallel in the Islamic states or the Far East. Universities arose out of concerns of the Church and the state in the twelfth and thirteenth centuries in western Europe. From the beginning, they were fixtures, and from the beginning, they needed extensive renovation. And yet, even despite this absolute certainty, universities have remained monolithic and static entities, renovating themselves just enough—but never more than enough—to avoid massive interventions by the state, the Church, or other elements in the system. Like parliamentary democracies, they function just well enough that while feelings of despair are frequent, and anticipation of imminent collapse constant, they continue. Some would say that they just limp along, and others would say they just carry on, because fundamentally they are strong and functional institutions.

Bill Readings, the Canadian academic who encapsulates the opposing point of view, argues that the role of the intellectual, which for him is the role of the university, is in doubt and failing at the end of the twentieth century.[2] The university as he constructs it arose from nineteenth-century Germany, from Wilhelm von Humboldt's idea that the purpose of the university was to inculcate a sense of culture both as a set of knowledge to be gained and a process to be implemented. That is, a university is a means of economic production, an engine for social change, a place of liberal enlightenment. In the modern era, Readings argues, the university is losing—or has lost—this purpose at its core, in favour of an instrumentalist production of graduates on the one hand and individual research in a set of silos on the other. It is time to acknowledge that the university is now posthistorical, a community of dissensus, a place where we think beside one another but with no integration into a community, into a *universitas*, into a joint understanding and consensus that will move us forward into the next generation of the university. Many would agree. I am not so sure. I wonder if there is not some value, as universities face a new set of challenges, in pondering the medieval university, the origin stories for the modern university, and the continuities that exist as much as do the fractures. Moreover, those continuities go back well beyond the Humboldtian notion of the originary construction of the university in nineteenth-century Germany, spreading from there very rapidly to North America. Where Readings follows Humboldt and sees only a rupture with Enlightenment and Rationalist traditions, I wonder if there are not underlying continuities with medieval origins and structures.

Parameters of this Study

The historical study of the university is not a particularly active field in the present day. Histories of individual universities do continue to be written, but in most cases they consider recent establishments, or they begin where a previous history left the story. The great tale of the medieval university remains the three magisterial volumes by Hastings Rashdall on *The Universities of Europe in the Middle Ages*, supplemented ably by Charles Homer Haskins, the historian who recuperated the twelfth century for modern study, in his *The Rise of Universities*.[3] A new general history in three (eventually to be four) volumes also offers a totalizing approach that begins in the Middle Ages in the first volume, and arrives at the Second World War with the third.[4] Most universities and colleges also have a faculty member or graduate who has devoted significant time to writing articles and books about the local history of that institution. That is, individual institutions tend to have useful analyses, at least up to the 1980s, when this subgenre perhaps peaked, but serious study of the university as an historical institution is nowadays scarce.

Moreover, the more general field of studying how universities developed in the Middle Ages has vanishingly few participants today. The absence of studies of the medieval university in current scholarship, however, is amply balanced by the astounding wealth of modern analyses of the state of the field. These analyses have three main trajectories: scholars in the field of education or one of the social sciences considering issues of policy, curriculum, and approach; former administrators offering fulsome considerations of their own approaches and sometimes more general analysis (most famously Clark Kerr and Derek Bok); and disgruntled or even furious faculty members offering views about the loss of academic freedom, the rise of the corporate university, the sufferings of contract faculty, the loss of faculty involvement in university governance, the failure of the liberal arts, the rise of neoliberalism, and the future of the humanities. These are all weighty and important issues, and they merit attention, but their proponents generally are not interested in how universities came to exist and to have the structure and function that they do today. Recent contributions in this field have also addressed the role of the MOOC (Massive Open Online Course); the shift to experiential learning, cooperative learning, work internships, and skills-based training; and the changing nature of student engagement in learning given the multitasking they engage in and the kinds of approaches to learning they nowadays find useful. The field itself has a great deal of internal debate and much passionate discussion. That said, however, the issue of university governance and the role of the university in society remains a specialist question in most modern societies. Only a few works in the field have gathered anything like a popular following. Whereas the health system and the school system up to the age of sixteen or seventeen are matters of broad public interest that receive frequent and passionate engagement in society at large, higher education still remains something of a closed book, a world known in pieces—its own highly personal and nostalgic pieces, as far as most students and former students are concerned—by those who attended a given institution or two, but not one broadly understood across society. If there is unrest at a particular university, only the students and alumni of that university, and perhaps the inhabitants of the town or city it is in, pay close attention. An outbreak of disease or a security issue in an elementary school draw much more attention from the media. A university's procedures and behaviour patterns are deeply encoded and more deeply codified, so that media professionals are usually stymied in their attempts to learn whether a particular issue might have general relevance or could be extrapolated to other universities or institutions. Where academics will happily talk about the health system or the environment or their scientific discoveries or pedagogy in the schools, they will generally not discuss their own institutions. Students will, and do, but their interventions are evanescent. In many nations and cultures the existence of a local, provincial, or national university will be a source of fierce pride, but one whose practices and approaches exist inside a black box. Taxi drivers point to the university as they drive tourists into town, and they indicate some of its buildings, but if they do speak of its quality of instruction or research, it is only ever in absolutely laudatory terms. In this respect, universities are remarkably medieval even today.

However, one thing that universities do have is a deep-seated sense of the medieval, whether recognized or not. In the modern day, the intellectual discipline known as medievalism is most often associated in the popular imagination with films, television shows, video games, and graphic novels with swashbuckling heroes, demure princesses, assorted nobility and royalty in chainmail or silks and satins, various monks and nuns delivering orders and messages, tournaments, castles, courtly love, medieval weaponry and warfare, and a general sense of the supposedly chaotic and colourful Middle Ages as the backdrop for the romance narrative unfolding in the text. The scholars who study medievalism, the reception of the Middle Ages, do tend often to focus on these more obvious signs of the medieval as it lives today. That is, the institutions and ideas that were at the core of medieval thinking are less flashy, and less likely to garner attention, even from scholars of medievalism. The study of medieval institutions and ideas is thus left largely to scholars of medieval studies, who tend to stop their work at the end of the Middle Ages.[5] Rare indeed is the sociologist, anthropologist, or historian of the university as an institution who begins as far back as its medieval origins and gradually moves forward to investigate the modern. Those who do this are mostly medievalists themselves: John Henry Newman (Cardinal Newman) in the nineteenth century, Jaroslav Pelikan, Astrik Gabriel, and Herbert Edward Salter in the twentieth century, and William Clark in the twenty-first century.[6]

Medievalism as a discipline is a relatively recent invention, and one with a good deal of ferment as it sorts out its main lines of argument and approach. There remains much disagreement, some of it productive and some of it simply fearful of being overrun by the cultural studies side of the house, which investigates the many modern medievalisms and neomedievalisms (following on initially from Tolkien studies, but now including J. K. Rowling, George R. R. Martin, and many modern fantasy writers and dreamers in software, manga, and videogames). In one noteworthy respect medievalism agrees with my approach here to universities. Because the study of the Middle Ages was largely undertaken during the nineteenth century, with the first editing of medieval manuscripts and the first synthesizing studies written about the Middle Ages all over Europe, medievalism involves awareness that our study of the Middle Ages is always implicated by the fact that we look through a lens that was first focused in the nineteenth century. We bring a romanticized view to the Middle Ages, because we are seeing them for ourselves but also through the lens brought to bear by the brothers Wilhelm and Jakob Grimm, William Morris, Gaston Paris, John Kemble, and other Romantic and Victorian figures. For example, our thinking about the Middle Ages in terms of nationalism, separating out the German tribes from the Frankish ones and both from the Norse, replicates nineteenth-century views of nationalism and ethnicity. Similarly, thinking about the modern university always nowadays starts with Humboldt and the rise of the research university in Germany, with its pattern being rapidly replicated around the world. Scholars of medievalism tend overwhelmingly to work on literary texts (and especially Anglo-American literary texts), although a strong minority addresses art history, religion, and science. There are indeed scholars of medievalism who address institutions, but their focus tends to be on physical or spiritual institutions: churches, monasteries, banks, the survival of Christian monastic orders, and the like. Few scholars today think seriously about the inherent medievalism in modern institutions, and none save Clark does so explicitly in terms of universities.[7]

My approach here will therefore involve a combination of medieval studies with medievalism; sometimes I will conflate the two, sometimes concatenate them, sometimes use medieval studies, and sometimes use medievalism. Perhaps some explanation of this complexity of approach will help. Occasionally elements of the medieval university survive to the present day, and sometimes elements of the modern university offer a kind of revivified medieval. These elements enact, consciously or unconsciously, a simulacrum of the medieval—a copy of an original medieval behaviour or structure that never existed. For example, the rituals of the modern university have a great deal of medieval panoply associated with them, especially including academic regalia. The regalia (robes, hoods, headgear) are often given great historical significance, and yet in most cases these insignia and other markers of university graduates—especially those achieving the academic heights of a doctorate—were actually developed in the nineteenth or even the twentieth century as something that ought to have been developed in the Middle Ages. The collection of academic peacocks at university convocations is a simulacrum, a copy of a medieval original that never existed. At other times medieval elements appear in the modern university by happenstance, simply a result of similarities in the patterns of human thought and behaviour. For example, students in modern universities declaring their agency and centrality to the university structure as purchasers of the services offered by the faculty, as clients, are replicating one of the medieval models of a university, that of the University of Bologna, perhaps founded in 1098. Moreover, they often combine forces with senior administrators in order to advance their agenda. These two groups wield similar kinds of executive power in the university structure, and they tend to want to leave similar kinds of legacies in the institution. The result, in the Middle Ages and the modern day, might be new playing fields for a sports team, new regulations about course offerings, career counselling centres, a new student centre for innovation and entrepreneurship (the last two perhaps more modern than medieval), or some other development in which their interests coincide. However, for my purposes here that coincidence of interests is not properly a feature of medievalism, but a simple replication of a medieval model. As a result, there will be considerable overlap here between the academic study of the medieval university, the academic study of the reception and reinstantiation of elements of the medieval university in the modern day, and the study of replicating patterns from the Middle Ages in the twenty-first century.

The principal question of this study—just how medieval is the modern university?—is not a simple one. Elements of the universities founded in the twelfth and thirteenth centuries in Europe survive in the modern university. Other apparently medieval elements have developed over the ages as a result of a medievalizing impulse. Disentangling these will not always be possible, but it will perhaps be possible to determine the ways in which the modern university maintains a fundamentally medieval structure and approach. In chapter 1, I will begin with issues of ritual and liturgy. Medieval or medievalist ceremonies abound in the modern university, as do the trappings of the medieval world. Universities have gonfalons and banners, coats of arms, and charming private traditions. They retain chancellors as their academic visitors or honorary leaders, and they delight in convocation ceremonies of great pomp and circumstance. The chapter will consider these rituals as elements of the liturgical structure of the university, and will address both the longstanding traditions of the Western university and the new rituals under development on a daily basis. Chapter 2 will turn to the structure of the university and consider ways in which it follows on from the medieval university, and ways in which it is returning to a medieval approach. The role of patrons, for example, is rich with medieval implications in the modern university as governments cut back their subsidies and insist that tuition charges must be matched by universities with massive scholarship options to ensure equality of access for all qualified students. As a result, the fundraising and advancement portfolios of a modern university have much in common with medieval donors and founders, and their ability to dictate elements of the colleges and universities they endowed. The roles of various senior figures in the modern university and the tricky political paths they must tread amongst academic senates and various structures of governing bodies also require examination from this point of view. Universities follow medieval ecclesiastical architecture, even in their newest buildings, and maintain an infrastructure that exactly replicates the push–pull of wanting to be a part of the community and wanting to maintain full autonomy as an independent institution. That is, the governance and physical structure of a university campus remains highly medieval in its approach and focus. Finally, chapter 3 will consider issues of teaching and the curriculum, considering the role of the student body and of the alumni. For example, recently the various European countries came together to attempt to ensure comparability in their degrees and in the quality of their education, producing famously a set of regulations known as the Bologna accords. One unintended consequence of the Bologna accords on teaching and learning in the university world has been a surprising sameness of curriculum, a smoothing out of difference. Governments around the world are attempting to establish transferability of credit. One reason for this is that students want that portability. Another reason is that if students can organize attendance at cheaper institutions of post-secondary education for part of a university degree program, that will allow governments to save considerable sums of money on their tuition and funding packages, and on their capital and operating budget transfers to the more expensive research universities, which might no longer be needed to teach first- or second-year students. The early results of the process have been a move in the direction of learning and program outcomes that are remarkably similar at every institution of higher education, and a potential return to the medieval model of portability, of courses taken at several different institutions with the degree taken at the most convenient final university. A second example with respect to the actual delivery of a university education is the issue of discipline and student welfare. To this day universities function as something of a world apart, subject to their own rules about behaviour and their own standards for health and welfare. The result can be an unexpected quantity of friction, as universities for privacy reasons cannot release to parents and relatives information about the mental or emotional state of a student, and often choose not to release information about punishment levied for various kinds of academic infractions or failures to live up to a university code of conduct. In this final chapter, then, I will consider some of the ways in which the putatively independent world of the modern university is steadily being eroded by quite medieval issues about discipline, conduct, and the curriculum.

Universities offer a fascinating lens on what society considers important. If a given society sends its best and brightest to its institutions of higher education, it presumably expects that those students will emerge at the other end of their studies fully inculcated with that society's values and ideals, aware of how to employ that society's beliefs and approaches, and knowledgeable about how to live well in that world. Not only should we consider the role of the university in every society, we should consider how that role has instantiated itself over many generations, and even over nearly one millennium. The extent to which the modern university is medieval offers, I will suggest, both cause for hope and cause for concern.

Notes

1 Jaroslav Pelikan, *The Idea of the University: A Reexamination* (New Haven: Yale University Press, 1992), p. 13.

2 Bill Readings, *The University in Ruins* (Cambridge, MA: Harvard University Press, 1996), p. 3 and *passim*.

[3] See Hastings Rashdall, *The Universities of Europe in the Middle Ages*, rev. ed. F. M. Powicke and A. B. Emden, 3 vols. (Oxford: Oxford University Press, 1936), and Charles Homer Haskins, *The Rise of Universities* (Ithaca: Great Seal Books, 1957). For smaller scale works that address more specific issues, see Robert Sangster Rait, *Life in the Medieval University* (Cambridge: Cambridge University Press, 1912), Helene Wieruszowski, *The Medieval University: Masters, Students, Learning* (Princeton: Van Nostrand, 1966), and Nathan Schachner, *The Mediaeval Universities*, rev. ed. (New York: Barnes, 1962).

[4] See *A History of the University in Europe*, vols. 1 and 2, ed. Hilde de Ridder-Symoens (Cambridge: Cambridge University Press, 1992, 1996); vol. 3, ed. Walter Rüegg (Cambridge: Cambridge University Press, 2007, online only); vol. 4 is forthcoming.

[5] For the relationship between medieval studies and medievalism, and their interaction with each other, see Kathleen Biddick, *The Shock of Medievalism* (Durham: Duke University Press, 1998), and Umberto Eco, *Travels in Hyperreality* (New York: Harcourt, 1986).

[6] See William Clark, *Academic Charisma and the Origins of the Research University* (Chicago: University of Chicago Press, 2006); Clark (not himself a medievalist by training) focuses on the material culture enacted by university lecturers, including disputations, card catalogues, lectures and lecture lists, appointment documents, and the rise of the doctorate, all in service of an argument tracing the role of the ascetic and charismatic professor, from Abelard onwards, but mostly from nineteenth-century Prussia, which for Clark is the origin of the genius entrepreneur-professor.

[7] Alice Chandler did, in *A Dream of Order: The Medieval Ideal in Nineteenth-Century English Literature* (Lincoln: University of Nebraska Press, 1970); she considers Henry Adams and his *Mont-Saint-Michel and Chartres* as both "the culminating work of the medieval revival; it is also the bitterest proof of its failure" (pp. 233–34). Two surveys of medievalism and its issues are Michael Alexander, *Medievalism: The Middle Ages in Modern England* (New Haven: Yale University Press, 2007), and David Matthews, *Medievalism: A Critical History* (Cambridge: Brewer, 2015); for some sense of the range of issues see *Medievalism: Key Critical Terms*, ed. Elizabeth Emery and Richard Utz (Cambridge: Brewer, 2014).

Chapter 1

Liturgy and Ritual

In May 2016, the University of East Anglia banned the tossing of mortarboards, citing safety concerns. At that university, the practice of ending a convocation ceremony with a spirited whirl of mortarboards into the air had become a beloved tradition. According to the administration, which together with the photographer handling graduating events provided a detailed explanation to the students of how they should mime the throw (the mortarboards would be photoshopped into the picture later), the issue was one of safety. The university also noted that damaged mortarboards were being returned to the rental agency. The most striking comment offered in response came from Louisa Baldwin, president of the Law Society at the university, who remarked, "If I've paid £45 to hire a bit of cloth and card for the day, I should be able to chuck my hat in the air! It's nothing worse than the weekly ritual of dodging VKs as they're lobbed across the LCR dance floor."[8] In other words, tossing mortarboards is a convocation tradition, and a part of the ritual of graduation that students thoroughly enjoy, even though all those mortarboards rising into the air have to come back down again, with their pointed corners stabbing into the heads, eyes, hairdos, and shoulders of the new graduates below. It's a tradition. It's a ritual. It's part of the liturgy of convocation.

Liturgy and ritual are terms that cause some disquiet in the modern mind, but they are fundamental to human endeavours. Rituals can be small ones, such as the tossing of mortarboards or the assembly of the right pens and pencils for the writing of an examination, or they can be extensive systemic patterns of behaviour that establish membership in a community, offer a sense of security and belonging, and provide an individual with faith for the present and the future. A liturgy is a formal pattern of behaviour with some fixed elements that are required in all repetitions of that pattern, and variable elements that depend upon the day of the year or the purpose of the particular enactment. For example, the liturgy that is enacted every summer day in North America is the baseball game. Those attending this liturgical event arrive at the cathedral and find their appointed place in the congregation (as previously determined by precedence and by preference), and enjoy the processions and elements of the opening sections of the liturgy: batting practice, the dancing antics of the mascot, the processional anthem, the required speeches about safety and sermons about the home team, the ritual exchange of the rosters, the introduction of the referees and the managers, and the offering up of the first pitch. The players take the field in their garb, which distinguishes them for the purpose of this enactment of the liturgy from the other team, and for the purposes of establishing the community of those involved with each team, their regalia is distinct from that of all other teams. The liturgy of a baseball game is fixed and immutable, and yet also surprisingly flexible. It has numbers and statistics, so that devotees of the liturgy can learn its higher aspects. It instantiates a narrative, and often a whole series of narratives, about individuals, about teams, and about the cities that sponsor those teams. Nowadays a second hymn is a requirement, during the seventh-inning stretch. A baseball game has a fully developed liturgy that provides a profoundly ritualistic establishment of community, embedding the game into the fabric of daily life. Moreover, the highly ritualized elements of a baseball game are highly medieval in their structure. The game has its unspoken codes and customs, and its progression through a sequence of repetitive events with a sense of steadily rising excitement, and with each instantiation of the liturgy having the same structure but different developments within that structure. A baseball game is a highly medieval structure, and a highly human one.[9]

The liturgy of a modern university is similarly a profoundly medieval element in its origins and in many cases in its development. For example, at most universities the *Academic Calendar* offers up the order of service for all elements of the academic experience of undergraduate and graduate students. The elements of the *Academic Calendar* are presented to students as a list of sessional dates reflecting the different deadlines, opportunities, and holidays of the academical year. At some universities, the pattern of the academic year is profoundly liturgical—Oxford and Cambridge still name some or all of their terms for Christian feast days of the saints: Michaelmas, Hilary, Trinity. Moreover, like any good liturgy, the dates in the sessional calendar are precise, the choice of behaviour and ritual on those days clear. Students must drop courses on a specific day if they do not wish the course to appear on their academic transcript. They must register for graduation by a certain date. The *Academic Calendar* offers them the details of their programs and of their courses, so that they know exactly what the requirements are for entering (matriculation) and exiting (convocation) their program of study successfully. Matriculation and convocation are themselves highly medieval in their conception, the opportunity in a modern university for a modicum of ritual, and sometimes a very large ritual indeed. Convocations come replete with all the trappings of liturgy: music, ceremonial robes and accoutrements, a mace, processions and recessions, the opportunity to petition for one's degree and receive it in a thoroughly medieval ceremony (often while kneeling to receive it), a fully developed hierarchy with the faculty—led by the chancellor—at the top, with the various echelons of graduating students arrayed in order and presented for their degrees according to a highly liturgical logic, and a profound underlying sense of the genuine significance of the moment. At many universities the pattern of the ritual explicitly embodies the change taking place in the individual: student at one end of the building, one side of the stage, tassel on one side of the mortarboard, and glorious graduate at the other end, side, or side of the mortarboard.

Writ small or writ large, the business of taking an academic degree is profoundly liturgical. That is to say, the rituals of the academic world are highly liturgical, methods by which a sense of solemnity and significance attaches itself to the business of attending a university. Learning and schooling in the modes that mark the university—lecture, disputation, tutorial, reading, and commenting—was already happening in the Classical worlds of Greece and Rome, in the Houses of Wisdom in Baghdad and many other places in the early Middle Ages, in the cathedral schools of Carolingian France, and in the monasteries and nunneries of Europe and northern Africa from the time of Augustine and especially of Benedict. However, although there is little study on this point, it is the ritual of the final examination and commencement that marks the medieval university as separate, that creates the business of knowing the *studium generale* and being ready to move on for further study to a *studium particulare*, return to the home monastery or cathedral, or obtain employment. In other words, the ritual of having one's learning confirmed by the masters of a university, the examination that creates a new master, is the ritual that is essential to the existence of a university, the one that involves processions and public feasting. The ritual of entering the university, of having one's name recorded on the role of a master, his *matricula*, is important for the structure and continuance for the university, and its ritual and liturgy are inward-looking. The outward-looking ritual is the final examination and convocation.

Ritual in the Medieval University Setting

University liturgy derives from two main sources: the origin of the universities in the religious culture of the middle and high Middle Ages, and the natural human impulse towards ritualistic behaviour at significant moments in an individual's life. University rituals today are a form of privileged action, reflecting as they do the ecclesiastical world of the early European university as well as modern preferences for spectacle and sensory pageantry. In the early university there were two principal rituals, both economic and social in origin. Students had to sign into the university system, joining one master and paying their fees to that master in a manner agreed upon in that university (and sometimes by extension with other medieval universities and institutions). When completing their final degree, they had to be admitted to the ranks of the masters, so that they could lecture without supervision or doctrinal oversight and collect fees for lecturing, and so that they could take pupils of their own. The latter ceremony was remarkably simple, and based on everyday behaviour: the new master, after defending himself publicly and either winning an argument or holding his own (it varied), would join the other masters at table for dinner. The masters' table was often slightly elevated by comparison with the scholars' tables, presumably so that the masters could see as necessary to impose discipline on their unruly charges (the history of the food fight is a venerable and highly medieval one). The new master would thus ascend to the masters' table and commence to eat there in common with his equals. Hence, he would eat at the *commensa*, the joint table, after his commencement ceremony of stepping upward—probably with guidance from other masters. He would, of course, already be wearing his ecclesiastical robes since all the members of the early university were members of the clergy, but the robes would be those of his religious order. What scholars of ritual studies call the "sensory pageantry" of such a ritual would probably in the early university be simply the opportunity to step up, to sit with more space, and to eat and drink well. Mention of such events in the annals of universities always do seem to indicate that the signal feature of the establishment of a new master was a banquet.

The new master had to wear correct garb from the moment of his advancement: academic regalia was by no means the colourful panoply that it is today, since it derived from the plainest ecclesiastical robe, the *cappa*. Since medieval scholars were obliged to be *clerici*, members of the clergy, they were expected to wear a simple version of clerkly vestments. The *cappa* was a voluminous cloak intended as outerwear, and was black and sleeveless, with a hood and sometimes a border of miniver around the hood and neck. (Miniver in the Middle Ages can be a generalized term for white fur, although in some areas it seems to specify squirrel fur or ermine, both in winter coats of white.) In the summer the warmer miniver hood or border on the *cappa* could be exchanged for silk. With a square cap—either floppy or fixed in shape like the modern mortarboard—or sometimes a small round cap (really a skullcap with some extra length at the top), the master was prepared for lecturing and for all official functions of the university. Students had somewhat more choice, though the ecclesiastical sense of hierarchy intervened enough that until they had completed their degrees they could not wear miniver; usually they wore the black capelet, shorter and with less volume than the *cappa* of the master. Robert of Sorbon was clear on this point in 1274 for his foundation, the College of the Sorbonne, decreeing that students must wear their outer garment, a *supertunicalia*, closed and should not have either furs of various colours or red and green silk trimmings on their cloak or hood. Plain garb would have to do.[10] His students at the newly founded college of the Sorbonne were all advanced theological students, and perhaps should not have had such frivolous urges anyway. But clearly, then as now, wearing the proper uniform, the liturgically required vestments of the office, was a necessity.

The commencement ceremony with which students joined the table of the masters initially had very little pageantry to it. Its most critical moment probably took place privately with the inscription of the name of the new master on the rolls of those entitled to lecture and to teach. Technically this matter was in the purview of the chancellor of the university (starting in Paris) but a master granted a chancellor's licence still had to be accepted by the masters in order to join the consortium, the *universitas*. The ceremony of inauguration as a master came to be called an inception, a ritual admitting the licensed master into the community; its parameters were often referred to in the university charter. Over time, symbols and other accoutrements were added to the basic structure. The examination to ensure the knowledge of the candidate came to have a fixed number of masters (three or four), sometimes agreed upon by the masters and sometimes with one or more appointed by the chancellor. The successful candidate sometimes read his name on a roll, and sometimes was the recipient of a candle, perhaps intended as a votive offering in thanks for the successful result and perhaps intended as a metaphorical or allegorical reference to the future master not hiding his light under a bushel. Sometimes all the masters had to agree on the successful candidacy, and elsewhere just a majority. Rashdall describes a "curious mode of voting" on the matter at Leipzig. Apparently the caps of the candidates were placed down the length of the table and each examiner would put a pebble into the caps of the rejected candidates, and a pea into the successful one. Then the peas and pebbles were counted, and the results determined.[11] One hopes that the peas were readily distinguishable from the pebbles.

By the fourteenth century this fairly simple ceremony had become a procession, with each candidate leaving from his hall or church, with the dignitaries of the central administration fore and aft (rector, proctors, bedel), and a brief collation (a formal lecture by the candidate) in the presence of the chancellor of the university before petitioning for the licence by kneeling in front of the chancellor. Save for the brief collation (nowadays given on behalf of all the graduates by a valedictorian or the recipient of an honorary degree, or blessedly dispensed with altogether), this ceremony pretty much replicates the modern convocation. The processions are shorter nowadays, and the practice employed by medieval students of expanding the procession by co-opting passersby to join in with the festivities has luckily ceased. Also, the students no longer have to pay for the feast: at universities that still offer such festivities to their graduating students, the banquet forms part of their tuition.

Matters were much more complicated at the starting point (and at the point in each year in which students re-registered to continue). The critical issue in the early university was to get the student's name on the rolls of benefice so that funding would come from the local bishop, or sometimes the pope or other ecclesiastical entity. To that end the new student had to obtain a place with a master, and to register for the required lectures. The period of study varied somewhat: in some universities students had to be twenty before they were permitted to take the examination to become a master; in others there was an intervening stage of a year or two, after which around the age of sixteen students took their first licence and began to study for themselves and not just listen to lectures. Basically, students had to establish themselves as members of the clerisy, which mostly meant the Roman tonsure, perhaps administered by the local barber for the poorer and lower-class students. Once at the university of their choice, they had to choose which masters to study with and determine their fees, while finding lodging and a community. Fairly rapidly the need for lodging developed halls and colleges, and also rent-controlled accommodations for those who did not join in with the more formal options. Joining the university was a simple matter of swearing an oath of obedience before the Rector (or sometimes the Chancellor) and paying the matriculation fees. As long as he kept paying the fees (and sometimes there was leeway on this point), the young scholar was entitled to an array of benefits. The first to lay out these benefits for scholars in the heady early days of university foundation was Frederick I, the Holy Roman Emperor more commonly known as Barbarossa, who offered a charter to the University of Naples (and also to Bologna) in 1158. The privileges of a member of the university included absolute security of their persons, in that no one was permitted to inflict any injury of any kind on a scholar or to bring about any loss to him. The penalty was fourfold restitution and revocation of the post. That is, were a local baker to short-change a scholar and be found out, he would have to provide four times the amount of bread free to the scholar, and he would lose his rights as a baker. Scholars also had the right to insist on a hearing inside the university, before the scholar's professors or the bishop, rather than in the civil courts. Barbarossa gave scholars the highly privileged place they hold today, and did so, one suspects, for the highly practical reason that the universities in his domains attracted many foreigners with their revenues, trained the people he needed to run his

government and church, and could be used for good public relations since they would sing his praises and be wholly
loyal to him and his heirs. Barbarossa was the first great
patron of universities, and in his case, he achieved his primacy of place without expense to his own purse. All he did
was issue a charter placing students and masters in a privileged sphere. So privileged was this sphere, in fact, that it
gave scholars more rights than the clergy. It took some decades and a lot of effort before the Church managed to gain
back that ground and establish itself as having the same
rights as the semi-autonomous universities it needed to try
to control.

Arrival at a university had become a grand event by
the fourteenth century, with formal and informal initiation
ceremonies. The new student, after matriculating with a
master, was a *bec jaune* (yellow beak, the equivalent of a
green-horn), a term that collapsed into a "bajan," and his
initiation involved a good deal of tomfoolery, a large feast at
his expense, some corporal punishment (blows with a frying
pan from the Rector, the Treasurer, and the Promoter at Aix,
for example), and a general sense of the new student being
the low man in the institution, available to serve his elders
and give them primacy of place.[12] There were national differences: at French universities the bajan was treated as a
sinner needing purgation, whereas at German universities
he was perceived rather as a wild beast. The basic treatment
remained quite similar, however. A pattern of highly ram-
bunctious behaviour was set: students who offended other
students in some way would, for the slightest infraction, be
obliged to pay a fine, usually in drink. This requirement was
called "sconcing," and elements of it remain today in the
tradition of "pennying" and other customs that randomly
impel the greater consumption of alcohol. Entry into the
life of a university student perhaps no longer requires an
expensive feast, but in many locations it still requires formal

and informal orientation ceremonies, with initiations also for special groups (fraternities, sororities, athletic organizations, and residences or colleges), and inebriation. Such traditions are sometimes driven underground, and in the current era attempts to eradicate them are underway, but they are rituals of initiation that allow the new individual to join the collectivity. Such rituals are difficult to eradicate altogether.

In fact, rituals fairly rapidly multiply. The early university, developing as it did out of monasteries and minsters, quickly developed a love of ceremonies. The early statutes of Paris reject any festivities on the admission of students, but insist that if a student in arts or theology should die, fully half of the masters must go to the funeral—and the other half will go to the next funeral. By 1231 there were more such events: a chancellor was to be installed by a bishop or in the chapter at Paris, with extended regulations:

> each chancellor, appointed hereafter at Paris, at the time of his installation, in the presence of the bishop, or at the command of the latter in the chapter at Paris—two masters of the students having been summoned for this purpose, and present on behalf of the university—shall swear that, in good faith, according to his conscience he will not receive as professors of theology and canon law any but suitable men, at a suitable place and time, according to the condition of the city and the honor and glory of those branches of learning, and he will reject all who are unworthy without respect to persons or nations.[13]

On the model of Paris, Rupert Count Palatine founded the University of Heidelberg in 1386. By that point he could specify that Heidelberg would be "ruled, disposed and regulated according to the modes and manners" of the University of Paris.[14] The one rector governing the university would obtain oaths from all the masters and teachers concerning their willingness "to observe the statutes, laws, privileges, liberties, and franchises of the same, and not reveal its secrets." The masters and bachelors were also required to move about, lecture, and exercise any scholastic function garbed in caps and gowns "of a uniform and similar nature." What was in the twelfth century something of a developing standard was by the end of the fourteenth a set of detailed and fixed protocols.

The Lecture and Classroom as Ceremony

Many rituals collect in the classroom: students pulling out their pens and paper or their computers (or these days their smartphones) in case they might want to take notes, a faculty member at the front of the room desperately attempting to get logged into the university system in the five minutes remaining after the previous class ran long and clogged the exits, and then more desperately attempting to upload the university's online pedagogical system and any PowerPoint decks that need to run. Nowadays there is also a pause for a moment of ritualistic prayer that the system or software will not pick this moment to update itself. Students with queries or issues search out a tutorial assistant or a professor. Other students settle in to browse Facebook or Instagram, or to upload the movie of their choice, having used their clickers to sign in to indicate their physical presence in the room. Sometimes, if the computer gods have been kind, there will be music playing to set the tone for the forthcoming class. And mostly, as the seconds tick down to the start time, the class pauses, the professor pauses for another moment of prayer that all the technology will work correctly and that the ideas to be imparted have some coherence to them, and then the class begins. Much ink has been spent on the old-fashioned lecture and its failings, and some ink has been spent on arguing that the fifty-minute lecture is a venerable and useful institution. Less, perhaps, has been spent thinking about the history of the lecture and the university classroom.

From the earliest establishment of the university, there were two principal modes of teaching: the lecture, and the *practicum* or tutorial where small-group learning often took place. Lecturing was done by masters or by senior bachelors who had already taken their first examinations and were studying to become masters. It was highly regulated by the university statutes. Absent from the university statutes is the job of the master inside a college or hall, the master to whose roll a given student had subscribed. From the earliest charters it is clear that this relationship was the crucial one for a medieval student, and that the master was to engage in close supervision of the student. The college statutes, when they started to be written in the thirteenth century, suggest that close supervision involved discussion and analysis of texts, the origin of modern small-group learning in the university context: tutorials and laboratory work. Also clearly a fundamental part of the early university's system of instruction is the disputation, the practice of debate, which combines the arts of the trivium—rhetoric, grammar, and logic— into dialectic. But the lecture, the sage upon the stage, was the heart of the university, the core of the endeavour.

Lectures were held at very fixed times, and it was the content that was the critical factor. Masters who wished to lecture on Gratian's *Decretum*, the central text of canon law, would do so at a fixed time of the day, generally around midday, whereas those lecturing on the basic texts of rhetoric would start their classes at six in the morning. Students were to have read the text, but it hardly mattered if they had, since the lectures—especially those for beginning students in the first three or four years of study—entirely consisted of hard, close reading of the text. The critical thing students had to bring with them was a copy of the text, which was much harder to come by in the Middle Ages than it is today.

During the lecture they would add marginal notes to the top and sides of their copy of the text, and references to other texts at the bottom of the folio (as footnotes). Sometimes they would add interlinear notes but mostly the school texts for study at the university were written in a small bookhand, and sigla would point to notes in the margin offering explanations of the text, disagreements with its purport, or further ruminations of various kinds. Senior students in the bachelor's program would in their fifth or sixth year be permitted to offer some of these lectures, although university statutes tended to enjoin them that they could not provide their own opinions or ideas, just provide the prevailing wisdom on Aristotle's *Ethics* or the *Metaphysics* or whatever other base text was designated for that lecture. In fact, the regulations surrounding the teaching activities of the senior undergraduates, the ones preparing themselves to become masters, sound distinctly like the activities of tutorial assistants today. The lack of faith and lack of trust in their abilities was, of course, germane only in the early university system.

There was some flexibility in the university system of lectures. Notably, a very popular lecturer could engage a lecture hall wherever and whenever he wished, and charge whatever he wished as well. Abelard, when teaching at Paris in the very early days of that university, did not hold a licence and at times moved out of the city, only to be followed wherever he went by students wanting to hear him. The early development of Bologna as a university specializing in law owed itself to the charisma of Irnerius, whose lectures were reportedly mesmerizing. Robert Grossetête, the first chancellor of the young university in Oxford, and his younger colleague Roger Bacon famously brought rigorous scholarship to bear on science; the former, however, had the knack of remaining on the right side of the church doctrinal authorities, while Bacon did not. Bacon was, it has to be admitted, the classic example of the irreverent academic willing to lash out at all unreasonable and ridiculous behaviour. Sadly for him, academic freedom was not a principle advocated in the Middle Ages. These lecturers established, through their abilities and their knowledge, the lecture as the core method of teaching in the European university. They also established the firm liturgy of the lecture: the time was set, often for generations; the lecture hall itself was sacrosanct (once a given lecture hall was in use, statutes in many medieval towns required that the house in which that hall was located had always to be available as a lecture location, thereby driving down the rents that the owners would be able to charge), and the pattern of teaching was established. Students prepared for the lecture by copying or arranging for copies of the primary material, and they wrote, by rote, the immortal words of wisdom handed down by the lecturer as commentary on the text. The fundamental ritual of medieval teaching was close reading of texts. Students learned the texts, by dint of much repetition and commentary. They did not learn a lot of texts, as will be discussed later, but the texts that they learned, they learned well.

Differentiating the University—Even More: New Ceremonies and Rituals

Pomp and ceremony have always been a part of the university experience. Wearing robes to lecture continues to this day in some universities, as does attending celebrations that mark graduation, matriculation, alumni returns to the university to celebrate their recollections of youthful follies, and other events specific to the individual institution (founder's days, notice of guardian saints, degree days of various kinds). Nowadays, these ceremonies are proliferating, both in frequency and in apparent meaningfulness. Orientation activities now include talks and opening lectures from the president and senior faculty. Pregraduation ceremonies include oath ceremonies such as the one at a business school handing out a gold ring for the graduand's pinkie-finger and enjoining ethical sensibilities and plans to build the future economy well. Homecoming in North American universities is no longer wholly about parades, a football game, various celebratory events, and many parties: now it has meaning, and is all about establishing a lifelong sense of community with each graduate. Donor relations intersect with alumni relations, and both involve extra celebrations: five-year anniversaries, fifty-year celebrations of a particular program or building, and various awards to individuals and groups. Moreover, although North American institutions have long held events to celebrate graduation from high school, the ceremonies are now proliferating, and include convocations from grade eight, grade six, and even kindergarten.

In the European context, ceremonies perhaps grew more organically. In the Netherlands, even today, the defence of a doctorate is a public event in which the candidate, who has already bound and published the thesis in over a hundred copies, arrives with the university bedel and answers questions for precisely one hour. The bedel comes thunderingly back into the room declaiming *hora est* (it is the hour) to end the ordeal. The ritual does not seem medieval, but post-medieval, yet clearly evoking a medievalist aspect. Gradual ceremonies are also becoming popular, so that students receive a matriculation feast, a commencement feast, and a second-year feast to mark the half-way point of the degree. Founder's day events and benefactors' events continue to proliferate, as does the practice of heraldry. Universities have coats of arms, flags, gonfalons, mottos, school songs, and more pomp and circumstance than they reasonably need. All of these elements create a sense of community.

In addition to the formal new ceremonies are the informal ones. The University of Texas at Austin has a remarkable new ritual called "Foam Sword Friday" that occurs on the last

Friday of each semester. Students wear costumes, the more outlandish the better, and they charge across streets or gardens (the location seems to vary somewhat, but mostly one crosswalk on the campus seems popular) and whack at each other with gray or pink foam swords. The swords resemble short foam pool noodles, although no doubt some are custom-made and have greater elegance to them. Slogans are written and sung, shouting is encouraged, and the students expend a great deal of energy. Foam Sword Friday is now embedded in the university culture and managed by the Center for Student Life, having originated among architecture students in the mid-2000s.

At Merton College Oxford, a ceremony dating from 1971 requires that Merton students in academical dress arrive in the Fellows' quadrangle at 2:00 a.m. on the day that Greenwich Time turns back one hour, and for the ensuing hour they walk backwards, arm in arm, around the quad and drinking port, completing their efforts to combat the temporal vortex at 2:00 a.m. when the hour is done. Originally a secretive ceremony eschewing publicity, the Merton Time Ceremony is now a well-known Oxford eccentricity.

In Canada in 1922, a group of senior engineers decided that they wanted to have a ceremony to call engineers to their profession, a ceremony separate from the formal accreditation they would receive upon graduation, but one which would be available only to students on the point of completion of their degrees. In order to develop a liturgy for the ceremony that would call engineers to a sense of the social responsibilities of their profession, they called upon Rudyard Kipling, who enthusiastically developed both a short statement of obligation and a ceremony. Also called the Kipling Ceremony, the Iron Ring ritual in Canadian universities provides the graduands with a ring to be worn on the little finger of the engineer's working hand. Lore of the ceremony states that the rings are made from a bridge that collapsed in Quebec, but in fact they are made of stainless steel, since iron corrodes and discolours. The ceremony is a closely guarded secret and Canadian engineers treasure their iron rings and the ritual associated with them.

These examples of new rituals, both informal and formal, clarify one element of university culture. Most university students are young, and their time at university can be transformational. They are still establishing their patterns of behaviour and figuring out what they will do with their lives, so the four or so years that they spend at universities often take on iconic significance in their memories and in their development. The friends they make at university are their friends for life, and the moments they share become fodder for laughter and for nostalgia for many decades to come. This pattern certainly begins in the Middle Ages, when students could be even younger than they are today, arriving at the age of thirteen or fourteen and staying through the formative years of their lives. However, also significant in these rituals is their medievalist appeal. The architecture students at the University of Texas at Austin needed to cut loose and work off some of the excess energy generated during their final examinations, and they came up with a medieval joust (really a *mêlée*, an inchoate mashup of warriors without a clear objective in the earliest such tournaments). They now brandish their foam swords and utter boasting words (in medieval literary terms, they engage in a *flyting*, although a proper *flyting* requires a boast from one individual representing one group of warriors and a response from the opposition) before racing together in battle formation. In 2012, one student narrowly escaped injury from a local bus that intervened on the battlefield (all battles have their unexpected moments), but this outpouring of energy and anxiety could not be cancelled, so now it is formally accepted as part of the university experience at UT-Austin. That is, a ritual demanded by the young students to work off steam is now imbricated into the university's ritual system. The Time Ceremony has had a similar trajectory, at one point frowned upon by the fellows of Merton but now accepted as a feature of the college, a quirk that allows the students to establish their community and reinforce their social connections. It helps that Merton has returned to academic heights of great splendour, as adjudicated by the Norrington Table for the finals results at Oxford. For the engineers who wear the iron ring in Canada, it has profound significance and marks their entry into their profession more thoroughly and more significantly than the graduation that follows within months. In other words, these new ceremonies have meaning, and they allow a ritualistic expression of that meaning that appeals to each student.

New Liturgies?
The Liturgies of Discipline and Planning

The story of how a medieval university first acquired its charter is told often. A German student at the University of Paris sent a servant boy from his rooms to a nearby tavern for more beer. The tavern keeper refused the office or provided a poor product, and in the ensuing attack on the tavern and over the next few days of tumult, the student and one or more of his rowdy fellows died. The provost of the city of Paris considered the students to fall under his jurisdiction, while the masters of the university, on this matter of governance completely united with their students, did not. They threatened the king that they would leave if he did not give them a royal charter exempting masters, students, and servants from secular jurisdiction. Philip Augustus, no fool, provided the charter in 1200. Matters did not end there. In 1229 there was a further extended altercation, also a result of a brawl between students and locals, this one over a failure to provide a sufficiency of a rather nice wine. The result was a two-year strike by the university against the town. Some students went elsewhere, and the masters hunkered down to await the arrival of sufficient privileges. After protracted negotiations they obtained a papal privilege confirming their exemptions and offering some more specific regulations about student attendance at lectures being required if they wished to continue to enjoy the relevant exemptions and the regulated price for lodgings. The university in 1231 was already a fully fledged corporation, carrying licences from both king and pope. Moreover, the University of Paris obtained these charters, which were quickly copied by universities already established in Europe and those that ensued, by exerting the economic and intellectual power of the *universitas*, the collection of students and masters who lived and studied in the Left Bank, the Latin Quarter. In so doing, they acquired charters that referred not to land or to buildings, but to a wholly amorphous entity, a collection of individuals. They were not obligated by the king or the pope to provide any service in return—just to continue to do the job of education in which they were already engaged. That is to say, from the earliest conflicts surrounding universities derived a very clear sense of the autonomy of the institution. The masters and students could largely do as they chose. Their business was to be a community, a *universitas*, a university.

This sense of the university as a largely autonomous institution continues today. Indirectly it derives from the generosity of Constantine, the emperor who fostered the continued existence of Christianity at the beginning of the fourth century. He seems to be responsible for deciding that churches and their assigns (monasteries, other religious institutions including universities) not only did not have to pay property taxes, but could accept and continue to hold gifts in perpetuity as untaxed charitable donations. Universities are thereby seen as a public good in most, if not all, countries, and in addition to the tax exemption and the opportunity to be a charitable institution, they also partake of a kind of limited autonomy. Following on from the medieval model of the university charter, student transgressions are treated differently. Most universities have their own codes of conduct and internal disciplinary systems. Some have separate codes for academic conduct and for conduct outside the remit of the classroom but inside the university. Plagiarism cases go to one tribunal, issues of drunkenness on campus to another. These separate disciplinary codes reflect the ecclesiastical benefit that accrues to universities; their denizens receive what is essentially the medieval benefit of clergy. Students who might have to face criminal courts for harassment or destruction of property instead present their cases to a university official and can generally appeal to a tribunal. The charter provided to the University of Paris by Pope Gregory IX in 1231 explicitly provides that "We command, moreover, that the bishop of Paris shall so chastise the excesses of the guilty, that the honour of the students shall be preserved and evil deeds shall not remain unpunished."[15] That is, university students answer to the bishop of Paris and not to any secular authority. There is some consideration of the town: "Moreover, we prohibit more expressly the students from carrying weapons in the city, and the university from protecting those who disturb peace and study."[16] Town and gown disagreements started early, and although they continue today, rarely does a university president nowadays have to insist that students not carry weapons in the city. (Statutes in some universities prohibited the carrying both of small weapons and of musical instruments.) Attempting to keep the peace and allow others to study remained a problem, however, throughout the Middle Ages. Early disputes between students and citizens generally had to do with over-celebration of festivals, as do many such disputes today. On this front, little has changed.

Moreover, universities established their own internal police forces very early indeed. At Oxford, through the centuries every Michaelmas term students have received their copy of the *Proctors' Memorandum* containing "general information including regulations relating to the conduct and discipline of junior members of the University."[17] The memorandum offers regulations on academic dress, dates of term, the rules respecting the syllabus for each course, and the rules of decorum applying to the sitting of examinations, as well as more recent rules concerning motor vehicles, the establishment of university clubs, and obtaining the necessary insurance and injections for foreign travel. Much is new, including regulations on parking, cyberspace, and sexual violence, but a surprisingly large *tranche* of the twelfth-century practices of the university proctors and assessor remains. That remnant no doubt infuriates the security professionals who must now interweave the protection of the university's physical and virtual campus much more fully into local and national security organizations, and find dealing with unruly students and faculty members steadily more tactically difficult.[18] More significantly, that benefit of clergy reflects an implicit patriarchalism and sexism, as students who might find themselves in the criminal courts for stalking or for date rape are able to offer confession and penitence inside the ecclesiastical courts of the university, and avoid the rather more trenchant justice that awaits outside the gates.[19] In this respect, the question of discipline on the campus, universities the world over remain resolutely medieval in their approach.

Universities do have a long-standing affinity for documents. The University of Paris went on strike for two years waiting for a charter that would enshrine its privileges. Other medieval universities demanded clear charters and statutes from kings and from popes, and sometimes from local bishops as well. They understood the value of written documentation. When the first strategic plans started emerging as documents sanctioned by the various governing bodies of universities (both academic and administrative) about thirty years ago, they were a very natural step. They affirmed the tradition of what the given university had always been, often with a brief historical excursus, and established ways forward to continue and improve on that tradition. Campus masterplans organizing what should go where and why have their roots in medieval college plans (universities were far less interested in the built space than were the colleges that had to feed, clothe, and find lecturing space for their masters). Modern documents of this kind follow directly in the track of their medieval predecessors.

Conclusion

Some university ceremonies and rituals survive from the earliest medieval universities, changed through the years but genuinely recognisable for their original intent and accomplishment. The lecture and the disputation still exist: the lecture altered away from the medieval model and is now altering back to it; the disputation has largely slipped to the edges of the undergraduate education and moved upwards in its application only to elements of achieving the doctorate, the highest degree available in the modern university. A potential doctor has to dispute for the degree. So also do charters and disciplinary rules remain, intact of themselves though with several additions for modern usage—and some would rightly argue an insufficient effort to understand the mores and customs of modern society. However, more obviously noteworthy are the apparent borrowings from the Middle Ages represented by the panoply and ceremony of many modern rituals, all of them belonging to the category of pure medievalism, and perhaps pure neomedievalism. These medievalist accoutrements—with the colourful plumage of the doctoral gowns, the revivified liturgy of the convocation ceremony, the flags and gonfa- lons, the ceremonial processions, and the music—all sug- gest the enduring power of ritual and liturgy, and especially the enduring power of a ritual and liturgy that invokes the nostalgic past. Thus, when students are piped into a com- mencement ceremony by bagpipers, or a marching band goose-steps its way into a chancellor's investiture banquet, or a university revises its motto or its typeface to look more traditional or established, these elements of medievalism and historicism serve to embed the university's new prac- tice into an ancient tradition—even where such a tradition actually does not exist. That is, many elements of the pomp and ceremony of the modern university are medievalism in its purest form, creations of a new medieval, simulacra of an original that never existed. That does not give them any less form or meaning, as the meaning of a ritual and a liturgy invests itself as time progresses as if it were an element always present. Universities establishing celebrations of founder's days, reinvigorating their school songs, or creating new mottos are partaking of this desire to embed current practice in an ancient past. The faster a university can make its new practices appear old and established, the stronger the practices and the more effective the establishment of a connection to the university will be. After all, establishing a connection to the brand and fostering that connection is fundamental to the continuance and growth of the univer- sity. The liturgies of discipline and autonomous structure of the modern university offer a clearer line of transmis- sion back to their medieval predecessors, but in the case of these documents universities generally present them as new and untrammelled by the past (except as something to be separated from, put behind). Despite their genuine con- nections to a medieval past, an antimedievalism inheres in these materials; universities want to be moving forward, to be reaching new goals, to be marching towards new frontiers. Thus, the obviously medieval trappings of the modern university are in many cases more medievalism than they are medieval studies, and the truly medieval elements of the modern university, such as the structures to be discussed in the next chapter, often have their medieval origins occluded.

Notes

[8] The decision received a lot of press: see http://www.theguardian.com/education/2016/may/18/university-ban-on-mortarboard-throwing-well-photoshop-them-in (accessed on May 18, 2016). VK is the brand name for a premixed alcohol drink very popular in the club scene, and apparently among undergraduates. LCR refers to the lower common room, the hangout area for undergraduates.

[9] Angela Weisl has written at length and very perceptively on baseball's medievalism, considering the sanctity, relics, and pilgrimage issues associated with a modern baseball saint, the slugger Mark McGwire, including his fall from grace. She also considers the redemptive story of Wade Boggs, who manages to shift medieval genres from *fabliau* to penitential confession, and redeem himself. See Angela Jane Weisl, *The Persistence of Medievalism: Narrative Adventures in Contemporary Culture* (New York: Palgrave Macmillan, 2003), pp. 40–120 at 121–41.

[10] For discussion and translated documents on this point, see Wieruszowski, *The Medieval University*, pp. 111–12 and 192–93.

[11] Rashdall, *Universities of Europe in the Middle Ages*, vol. 1: *Salerno-Bologna-Paris*, p. 460 n. 3.

[12] Many more details of the "jocund advent" are provided in Sangster Rait, *Life in the Medieval University*, pp. 109–23.

[13] See the very useful Fordham University website now called the Internet Medieval Sourcebook, with medieval source texts in translation, http://sourcebooks.fordham.edu/source/UParis-stats1231.html (accessed September 30, 2016).

[14] See http://sourcebooks.fordham.edu/Halsall/source/1386heidelberg.asp (accessed September 30, 2016).

[15] http://sourcebooks.fordham.edu/source/UParis-stats1231.html (accessed September 30, 2016).

[16] See http://sourcebooks.fordham.edu/source/UParis-stats1231.html (accessed September 30, 2016).

[17] *Proctors' Memorandum* (Oxford: University Printing House, 1983), front cover; nowadays online, https://www.admin.ox.ac.uk/proctors/info/pam (accessed June 6, 2016).

[18] A collection of essays that tells this story from the opposing position is *Policing the Campus: Academic Repression, Surveillance, and the Occupy Movement*, ed. Anthony J. Nocella II and David Gabbard (New York: Peter Lang, 2013).

[19] There are many striking recent examples of this problem, especially in North America. See, for example, Jon Krakauer, *Missoula: Rape and the Justice System in a College Town* (New York: Knopf Doubleday, 2016). Krakauer interweaves the tale of the University of Montana investigations and decisions with the police investigations and the two criminal proceedings that emerged from a whole sequence of rapes of young female undergraduates, many apparently by members of the football team.

Chapter 2

Structure

A student wakes up groggily, rolls out of bed, grabs some food, and rushes to a required lecture. It's been at the same hour since time immemorial, and attendance is mandatory. The lecturer is pretty well-known and highly regarded, unlike the stultifying stumblebum yesterday. A second lecture ensues. A few hours later, the student has a tutorial, and then some group work for a presentation. In between, the student might study, might rush to a part-time job, might hang out with fellow students, might engage in some physical activity or in one of many extra-curricular options. The tutorial, in a small group, will be supervised by another, often more junior, member of the faculty. The evening might be spent studying, but the student is young and the pub beckons enticingly. After all, this is the time to grow up, learn good patterns of life (by encountering and embracing the bad patterns for a while), and make friendships that will last a lifetime. At set times, there will be tests or examinations to see what the young student has learned. At some point, the student will have learned enough to sit final examinations and graduate. And another generation of students arrives for the same procedure. Other than the free time, which is more than would be permitted by any spiritual mentor, this is a highly ecclesiastical structure, and it is the basic structure of the medieval university. It is also, of course, the basic material of the modern university. We might wake nowadays to the warblings of a digital device, and more senior students will be hopping a bus or arriving on campus by way of personal transportation more sophisticated than walking, but the fundamental elements remain the same. Students are dislocated entities, having to figure out a new pattern of life, preferably very quickly, and engage in independent study (as little as possible—it's always good, and sometimes very smart, just to figure out what the received wisdom is as far as the professor is concerned, and just provide that, since it prevents both charges of heresy and low grades). Time at university is time apart, dislocated (even perhaps epiphanic) time, the opportunity to grow, to learn. That has not changed in nearly a millennium. Moreover, the basic pattern and structure of the university has changed far less than many modern commentators believe.

What connection, then, does the structure of the multi-versity of today have with the small group of colleges with one central administration building (often a very modest house) of the late twelfth century? Well, more than you might think, and on several axes. First, the two basic models of governance in the early university still pertain today, although nowadays their force and relevance can often be heavily occluded. In one model, the students are the centrepiece, the decision-makers, the focus and locus of power; in the other, it is the faculty who found and govern the university, deciding its priorities and offering its curriculum. Second, the highly ecclesiastical and hermetically sealed structure of the internal divisions of the university remains very similar indeed to its medieval antecedents. Whether they are organized in modern or medieval faculties, divisions, schools, or departments, the unitary structure inside a university reflects not the community or *universitas* but rather the self-motivated and internally consistent world of the monastery. Each unit is a silo unto itself, and each silo in a university exists in a silent but ferocious competition for power, for funding, for students with every other faculty. The colleges of Oxford and the faculties of Paris might well be rife with internal division and strife, but they fought to retain their foothold on power, their control of their own destiny, with remarkable tenacity and fierce concentration. Mention the strategic reallocation of funding to any department chair in a university today, and you will see the same quivering intensity of fear, anger, and avarice as there would have been in her medieval counterpart, along with the quick calculus of how this opportunity can be used to buttress her own scholarly field. Third, although much ink disappears to discussions of academic buildings and learning opportunities in universities, the sad truth is that universities did not become self-sufficient and autonomous entities until they embraced the concept of housing. There were, and are, simply too many vagaries and uncertainties of the fiscal variety that accrue to complete dependence on tuition as the sole revenue of the university. The government (or the pope or the prelate or the noble or the king) has to remember to send the funds on time to pay for all the scholarships and subsidized students. The paying students (always a surprisingly limited few; the sliding scale of tuition charged according to means in the medieval period seems actually fairer and more sensible than modern funding packages) have to pay up on time, and not start negotiating about the details. The good burghers of the city or town who are offering tax breaks to the university might capriciously decide to make greater development charges, or come up with an ingenious way to put a large roadway right through an area the university considers sacrosanct. Donors can be a strong source of income, but also a somewhat uncertain one, as whenever the economy goes south it takes donations south right along with the central funds from the treasury, concomitant with the increased local taxes. However, once a university gets into the business of the college and starts to house and feed the young undergraduates, or finds a similar budget line (conferences, offering sanctuary for the king's household during a period of unrest, retreats and symposia), a permanent revenue stream of inestimable value establishes itself. Universities that do not have sufficient housing revenue have to scramble, and indeed also had to scramble in the Middle Ages. Fourth, establishing the right location and getting the physical university started is critical. At least the first few buildings need to be up, each with three to four floors, quirky collegiate architecture, brick or stone to indicate permanence, a coat of arms or motto carved to make a liturgical link to the past and a harbinger of the long future, some grass and landscaping with foliage around to make the ecclesiastical link to greenery, an emphasis on light, with large or frequent windows (or both), and possibly a tower, a spire, or some other clearer sign that this is an important entity, with spiritual and intellectual aspirations, and with a sense of permanence and reverence pervading it. These are the basic structures of both the medieval and the contemporary university.

Structural Systems of the Medieval University

In the Middle Ages two quite different university structures were in play, both of which survive, in principle at least, to the present day. One is by far the most popular nowadays, but the other remains a striking option, and one that is perhaps gaining significant traction in the modern era. The pattern at the university of Bologna (in many traditions the first university, founded in 1098) has a group of students banding together and commissioning a master, a professor, to offer them lessons on a subject of their choice. They choose their material and their teacher, and oversee their own system of learning. The pattern in Paris and Oxford is for masters to organize sets of lectures and to oversee further focused study, interviewing and recruiting students to a system of classes organized by the lecturers. Thus, Robert de Courçon's early statute at Paris explicitly requires particular texts: the treatises of Aristotle, the two Priscians, Boethius. It explicitly excludes the work of David de Dinant and that of the heretic Almaric, Maurice of Spain. In 1215, Robert states very clearly that "Each master is to have jurisdiction over his scholars."[20] While masters and students can make other kinds of agreements and regulations, this is the base, and no student can be at Paris without a regular master. Bologna, on the other hand, offers a more parlous existence for the tutor and lecturer. As R. W. Southern points out, "[o]nly a very able or well-endowed master could live on the fees or gifts of his pupils; the remainder had to push out into the world to seek preferment at the hands of men whom they could serve."[21] This system did endure in some respects: students at Bologna and its daughter institutions (mostly Italian) today still have greater power than is the norm in European universities—and indeed all universities. In other respects, however, this pattern was not a lasting one. Even at Bologna it rapidly becomes clear that the agreements establishing the relationships between the city and the university are those between city officials and the masters of the schools, both of them free to act as they choose. The merchants of Bologna value the accomplishments and financial worth of having popular and highly qualified masters teaching at their local university, and they negotiate and work with them to confirm and extend the connection between town and gown.

Many of the basic elements of both patterns remain today. Universities largely continue to believe that they are autonomous, equal, and independent institutions that happen to find themselves in existence in a city. The masters of the University of Paris successfully appealed to the king when the city of Paris was attempting to impose rules and regulations on the unruly students in the Left Bank. They threatened to leave, to shake the dust of Paris from their feet and move their illustrious selves—and with them, their well-endowed and freehanded students—elsewhere, as they had several open invitations. They also demanded, and received on behalf of most masters at all European universities, the *ius ubique docendi*, the right to teach anywhere, from the pope, as confirmed by various ecclesiastical authorities in later generations. That is, from the earliest times the masters and scholars at universities insisted on their rights and privileges, on their portability and their autonomy. These early developments had a tremendous effect on the important structures of the university: its governance (the role of the chancellor as against that of the rector—later, in many universities, the president—or the issue of the governing council of faculty members and its somewhat democratic decision-making), the different methods of founding a university and advancing it, the external context of patronage and politics, the internal context of colleges and halls, and issues associated with finances and buildings. First, however, the two principal models for university structure merit further attention.

Bologna and Paris

The earliest model for a European university was run by students. In Bologna, some evidence suggests that the ancient Roman tradition of law continued to be studied, along with the juridical traditions of Lombardy or northern Italy. Thus there seems to have been, in the eleventh century, an episcopal school, a monastic school and a municipal school stressing the teaching of rhetoric (in order to argue about the law). These existing sources were galvanized in the twelfth century with the superb teaching of Irnerius (also called Werner or Guarnerius) and the work of Gratian, a monk from a monastery in Bologna who produced his *Decretum*, the seminal work codifying canon law (church law). Both Irnerius and Gratian organized and codified their material, advancing the underlying principles of law and legal thinking in hugely original and useful ways. Their work was seized upon in Bologna by communities of students. It was students who organized themselves at Bologna, and worked together to choose and hire masters to teach them. The governing authority of the nascent university was technically a rector, elected to serve for a year by the outgoing rector, the *consiliarii* (leaders elected by the various learning communities), and by the general congregation of students of the university. The masters did not have a vote. As a result, they collected in their own groups and gradually gained some power and authority over the ensuing centuries. The rector was largely an administrative figure simply applying statutes and collecting fees and fines; his principal qualifications were that he was to be a student of about the age of twenty-five, and his secondary qualifications, since he was obliged to feast the entire community at his inception, were wealth and generosity. He could adjudicate disputes and supervise issues to do with housing and relations with the town. His officials had some control over the lecture schedule and its application, but it was the students who determined the curriculum and chose the masters, hiring and firing them at will, determining what they should lecture on and when, and intervening as they chose in the functioning of the university. A master needing to leave his duties for a few days had to have the permission of the rector, and if he needed to leave for more than a week, he needed the permission of the entire university. Moreover, he had to leave a sum of money as surety against his return. It was quite possible that, while he was lecturing, without asking for permission a bedel or proctor would enter the room and interrupt to deliver a message having to do with the functioning of the university, because the lecturer did not have the right to deny it. The structure of the university was the structure developed by the student bodies. They even required that the masters lecture on one chapter at a time, and proceed logically through the books they were teaching, systematically, without skipping over any difficult materials or leaving them to the end of the lecture. The students could intervene at will, since they were the ones with the economic power, with the right to hire and pay the faculty. Were the students to boycott an individual master's lectures, he would be destitute.

Some have suggested that students of civil law, the principal focus of study in the university at Bologna, tended to be already older and more judicious, and more capable of identifying and hiring the correct faculty for their needs. There is certainly some truth to this argument, as students in the Faculty of Law tended to be in their twenties, and to be aware that their education was bringing a kind of general understanding of the rule of law to all the European states. To acquire a degree from Bologna was accomplishment indeed, and tended to result in a senior post back home, with much opportunity for further advancement. Even so, as time went on it is clear that the rector and the faculty together gathered more power, and the student structures lost theirs. Nonetheless, a surprising number of Italian and other Mediterranean universities today have a significantly stronger role for students in the governance of the institution than is the norm elsewhere. On the other hand, students in the modern era seem in a surprising number of universities to have achieved a Bologna-like level of engagement in the university. That is, the modern construction of the student as client, as purchaser of services, as acquiring a commodity that is a university diploma seems to replicate in intriguing philosophical ways the Bologna system of students choosing and paying for the commodity that is a set of lectures.

University presidents and senior administrators lunch with the presidents of the student bodies (their counterparts), and together they reach policy conclusions that are later brought to the governing bodies of the institution as matters already agreed upon. In this model, quite common on several continents, students are policy drivers, and they consider themselves the single most important "stakeholder" in the university, the group that ought to have a majority vote on senior governing bodies. They are, after all, the clients, the purchasers of services. If the university functions as a kind of government these days, student organizations are non-governmental organizations with direct access at the highest level to policymakers, and a very strong willingness to make use of that example. Their attempts to rule over the delivery of material (make all classes available on podcasts, require that those marking their work provide extensive justifications and allow resubmission, add extra days for study to the term, and delete teaching days) are not surprising. After all, in Bologna, they reigned.

The Paris model was an assembly of masters, not an assembly of students. As Charles Homer Haskins puts it, "[a] university in the sense of an organized body of masters existed already in the twelfth century; by 1231 it had developed into a corporation, for Paris, in contrast to Bologna, was a university of masters."[22] By this point the university had also developed four founding faculties, each with a dean, in arts, canon law, medicine, and theology. The Faculty of Arts was by far the largest, and theology—although this was the faculty at Paris with the greatest renown and the greatest impact through history—was by far the smallest and most exclusive. Law and medicine were additions for completeness, but probably not borne out of the cathedral schools the way the original university was in the middle of the twelfth century.[23] The story of that university's origins we have by inference and by records of conflict and their resolution in statutes. As the first students were attracted to masters teaching on the Ile de la Cité, they came into conflict with the chancellor and chapter of the Cathedral of Notre Dame, who considered that this new and more advanced school, reaching towards autonomy, needed to fall under the hegemony of the Church. The struggle for independence was protracted, and many other issues muddied the waters. For example, the horrifying treatment of the scholar and teacher Peter Abelard at the hands of his lover Heloise's uncle is perhaps coloured by the fact that Fulbert was a canon of the cathedral, and one of those anxious to control these upstart masters whose lectures were so beguiling to young minds and so potentially heretical and dangerous as far as the Church was concerned. Other apparently random decisions also affected the early history of the university: in 1257 the king of France, Louis IX (the only canonized king of France, Saint Louis), gave his personal chaplain Robert of Sorbon (now called Robert of Sorbonne) a house and stables on the Left Bank, in the worst area of Paris, for him to establish a location for poor scholars to live and study. Two years later he expanded his donation to all the houses he owned in the same street; others donated as well, and Robert acquired support from the pope and successfully endowed his Congregation of Poor Masters. He was the driving force of the nascent college, fundraising for it, endowing it, developing its corporate organization, mortgaging the properties, and swapping lands and houses in order to establish complete academic independence for his institution. That is to say, the remarkable success that the University of Paris had in developing its autonomy owes itself partly to random chance in that it had spectacular lecturers, excellent organizers, absolute support from the king, and support from the pope who (as popes tended to be) was in conflict over taxes and emoluments with the local clergy. The result was a series of statutes and charters that endorsed the development of Paris as self-governing, autonomous, but also wholly supported by church and state. And, early on, it became a residential collegiate university, although not with the model that shortly thereafter became the most powerful example of the collegiate university, at Oxford.

In the Bologna model, power gradually collected in the hands of some longstanding executive officials, the individuals who were on the ground given that the student-centred model tended to lead to greater mobility of the faculty, and students by their very nature do, even if they take the prescribed sixteen years, eventually graduate and move on. In the Paris model, that power and financial control was always firmly in the hands of the masters. They controlled the executive and administrative branches of the university, and made the relevant decisions. Whereas at Bologna the larger body of all the students and voting members of the universities tended to be summoned to deliberate and decide on a wide range of matters, at Paris the members of the masters' guild met, when necessary, to determine policy and practice. Students at Paris were automatically members of the clerisy, part of the ecclesiastical establishment, whereas the terms of Barbarossa's statute for students in his jurisdiction gave them separate and exclusive status, neither clergy nor lay, but endowed with their own privileges. At Paris, they received the privileges of the clergy; this was the model that inhered in most, and eventually all, European universities.

One feature that was standard in the medieval universities, and was already present in both Bologna and Paris, is the way the students in the largest faculty, and to some extent in the other faculties, were explicitly segregated into "nations." For example, at Paris there were four nations in the Faculty of Arts—those of Picardy, Normandy, England (later more often called Germany), and France. Each arriving student joined a nation based on his home nationality, and the nations had their own semi-autonomous governing structures. These were detailed and generally democratic (sometimes random chance picked the leader, often called the proctor, of a given nation). At Bologna there were only two large nations by the time records are clear: the *ultramontanistas* (those beyond the Alps) and the *cismontanistas* (those on this side of the Alps, the Italians themselves). The only individuals barred from joining one of the two nations were natives of Bologna. It could be argued that this division of the medieval universities, at least at the level of the student body, is a sign of the acknowledged internationalism of the medieval university. That might be. However, it seems to me that this division into nations was more a way of separating out the students and not one of uniting them into a whole. While nowadays many universities have turned to international recruitment to bolster their financial situation, advance a global agenda, and engage in continued growth (on the theory that the modern university must always be growing), the tendency on many campuses to hold those international students sequestered is not a positive development. This creates a weirdly paradoxical situation of international students existing in their own small enclave in a foreign country and paying exorbitant fees for the privilege of attending a famous or high-quality (or just a different) university. The free exchange of ideas and cultures that this kind of exchange should foster does not always develop. While this does certainly constitute what appears to be an exact parallel to the way in which medieval universities functioned, with segregation of the nations into enclaves in the city as well as training offered by masters from the given nation, it does not for my purposes here seem a useful comparison.[24] The organization into nations is a feature that rightly broke down in the late medieval period. At Paris, once England had both Oxford and Cambridge, the English nation was renamed the German nation since they were now preponderant. And once the papal schism and the establishment of a second papacy at Avignon meant that it was cheaper and easier for German emperors to establish universities in that nation, the German nation also disappeared from Paris. The result was a significant diminution of the concept and power of the nations.

Salerno and Prague

Salerno has a very strong claim to make as the first true university, and an absolute claim as the first specialist university. Studies in medicine at Salerno (about thirty miles from Bologna and the two *universitates* do seem to have influenced each other's development and governance) began in the eleventh century. The nearby monastery of Monte Cassino had a foundational collection of relevant materials, and it also became the final home of Constantine, originally from Carthage but in his day the writer of many works on medicine as well as a practitioner of the medical sciences. He seems to have taught publicly at Salerno, along with monks from Monte Cassino, Jews, and possibly even some learned women. In about 1065, Salerno was granted privileges by the Duke of Apulia, Robert Guiscard (a Norman who had recently conquered Apulia and Calabria, and had also been treated at Salerno for a battle wound). By 1137, the charter had been extended by later rulers, who provided details concerning the need for state-ordered examinations in the field of medicine, leading to the delivery of a licence, called specifically a *licencia medendi*, a licence to practise medicine. Despite the impetus for its foundation being the highly learned monastery of Monte Cassino, Salerno appears to have had a largely secular history in the Middle Ages.

Prague appears here because it was the first university explicitly to be founded, and the first of many universities in what later came to be called the German system. The other universities discussed to this point developed somewhat organically from cathedral schools or monastic schools (or both), with a gradual move to public lectures and to establishing rules for students and for masters. Prague, however, was intentionally founded in the year 1348 by the king of Bohemia, Charles IV, first as a *studium generale*, and in the next year confirming in a charter all the rights, privileges, and immunities that a university expected to have in the middle of the fourteenth century. Charles IV was Holy Roman Emperor, and certainly knew that a previous Holy Roman Emperor, Frederick II, had proclaimed statutes for a university at Naples in 1224—but in that case he was confirming an already existing institution, not starting a new one from scratch. Frederick II also acted, in part, to offend the papacy, on purpose, by offering his support for the university as an entirely independent entity. Charles did not follow this approach, and had in 1347 obtained permission from the Pope, by way of a papal bull, and by way of the papal appointment of a chancellor, intended to be a ceremonial role and not one imbricated in the fabric of the university-to-be. Otherwise, he embarked on new ground, establishing the rights and privileges and structures of his university as a new-thought endeavour improving on previous structures. The four nations or four faculties each elected a dean, and a complicated but relatively democratic process elected a Rector, who administered for six months ensuring that statutes were followed and the university's property was preserved. While technically the salaries of the faculty were distributed by the Rector as part of the common property of the university, the four faculties also had their separate funding, from charges for the courses the students were taking. Students also paid fees directly to the masters whose lecture courses they were taking. They were obliged to complete at least a two-year bachelor of arts course before entering the professional faculties of law or medicine. A former student at Paris himself, Charles tried to combine its best elements with an administrative and curricular structure that was more streamlined. In that respect he was somewhat unsuccessful, as the Faculty of Law seceded from the other three almost immediately (keeping only the chancellor in common) and disagreements about the structure of the student nations led to the departure of the German contingent. However, the structure he established at Prague became the norm for the German universities that followed. Its statutes incidentally offer very precise information about the order of procession in public ceremonials, which suggests that at this point the public rituals of the university had achieved major significance. It is also perhaps worth noting that all the medieval universities appointed administrators (rectors, deans, even chancellors) for strictly limited periods of time, ranging from six months to a few years. Administrators were not encouraged to stay in post under this system, although—and this is perhaps not unexpected news to the observer of the modern university and its tendencies in this regard—they often did.

The pattern at Prague remains the typical one for founding universities in Europe: sponsored by the state or by local prelates with land and funding provided along with a strongly autonomous structure and function. In other words, from Prague onwards universities are often born entire as entities with close connections to the state and to local dignitaries. They certainly embark on growth, sometimes rapid growth, sometimes little growth for centuries thereafter. From the foundation of Prague forwards, universities have almost always begun with state charters or received state acknowledgement early in their development. Local dignitaries, however awkward the relationship with the university could become later on (and conflicts between town and gown began in the medieval period and continue to this day, though nowadays with less loss of life), also as a rule approved of the influx of capital and of free-spending students.

Perhaps the most intriguing point about the founders of medieval universities (where a specific founder can be identified) is the fact that these individuals did not thereafter have substantive academic control over the newly established institution. The academic decision-making, and indeed in almost all cases all the decision-making, passed directly into the hands of the masters. However grateful they might have been to their patrons, they negotiated with them as an independent and autonomous entity, and they seized control of their enterprise. William of Wykeham could commission and build New College, and endow it, but he could not govern it. Thomas, Cardinal Wolsey, could plan and build Cardinal College, later to be Christ Church College, Oxford, but the fellows of the college in the end determined its structure and purpose, and altered his plans for its enormous size. They wanted autonomy, especially from the Church but also from aristocratic and royal founders. For example, only a few founders succeeded in negotiating guaranteed entrance for "founder's kin." Those few that did generally lost the privilege after a few generations. This fundamental principle, that a given university governs itself and makes its own academic decisions about entrance, succession, and graduation, derives from the earliest medieval institutions. It does not appear to have been a hard-fought battle for control, but a recognition by both the Church (although the Church was more likely to attempt to intervene) and the state, in the form of various monarchs and patrons, that universities were a *universitas*, a self-governing community.

The External Context: Politics and Patronage

Modern universities tend to have policies surrounding their fundraising and advancement systems, policies that cover who they will approach as a potential donor, how to engage in the approach and build the relationship, vetting offers of support and doing due diligence on the potential donor, establishing the terms of the gift in light of university autonomy and other concerns, and continuing to curate the donor relationship. Unsurprisingly, medieval universities worked in precisely the same way, though perhaps without precisely the language of building a donor pipeline or pyramid. However, the *gaude* (Homecoming, Reunion Weekend, Alumni Day) was an early development, the welcome back to the university proffered to every graduate, linking them with the long stream of other engaged alumni. From the amounts of money spent on inception feasts for new masters and for heads of house or rectors, it would appear that recent graduates also came back for these events (the numbers fed are sometimes far greater than the highest possible estimate for current students in a given university or college). It also has to be said that medieval heads of house were perhaps more willing to skirt disaster in their search for funds, willing to make requests for money even at funerals or in moments of great stress, and they were also perhaps less scrupulous than modern fundraisers. Where nowadays fundraisers do some pre-vetting of potential donors, and politely shy away from those whose donations might raise ethical questions for the recipient, in the Middle Ages universities clearly accepted all comers. For example, one early Principal of Brasenose College, Oxford rather brazenly approached a widow at the funeral of her only son to suggest that she consider endowing places at his college for twenty students (alternative sons, he said). She was much struck with the idea, and indeed Jocosa Frankland gave liberally to two Cambridge colleges, and even more liberally to two Oxford colleges. Her son had died while a student at Gray's Inn in London, so Dean Alexander Nowell (he was also Dean of St Paul's and a Canon of Windsor) did not even have the foothold of the son's having died while at Brasenose to justify his approach.[25] That it worked is not, perhaps, a recommendation to the modern fundraiser to try this technique.

The first honorary degree (another part of the donor pipeline) seems to have been at the University of Oxford in 1478 or 1479, and seems to have been offered for the wholly venal purpose of currying favour with a great man of the time. Lionel Woodville was the Dean of Exeter and the brother-in-law of Edward IV, part of the clan of Woodville children who surrounded Edward after his surprising marriage to the eldest of the thirteen, Elizabeth Woodville. Before his death in 1484 he was also bishop of Salisbury and chancellor of the University of Oxford. Woodville did hold a bachelor's degree in canon law, but he was offered the highest possible degree *honoris causa*, as a result of his honour and without any suggestion that he fulfil the usual requirements of the degree. The period was the middle of the Wars of the Roses, and acquiring Woodville's patronage may well have seemed a clever move. The notion of the honorary degree resurfaced about a hundred years later, and reached a low point when Charles I moved his court to Oxford and convinced the university to offer about 350 honorary degrees to the members of his court and others he wished to acknowledge. The university objected, not so much on intellectual or ethical grounds, but financial; since none of these recipients had paid their regular fees to the university, no benefit accrued to the university's coffers for honouring the individuals in question. Perhaps this is the origin of honouring individuals who might afterwards be cultivated as potential patrons of the institution. Universities do like their degree holders to pay for the privilege.

What this first honorary degree also points to is the difficult position universities are in with respect to the political world of a given age. Fairly rapidly, and quite intelligently, universities became bulwarks of the state and the Church, offering support and also providing incubators for new ideas and serving as places that advanced the ideas of the political leaders of the day. Because universities had a monopoly on certifying intellectual knowledge and expertise (a monopoly that largely persists today), they became central to offering advice to church and state. In some respects the universities became the great supporters of the Church in the later medieval period, bastions of conservative ideology. From their earliest days they had highly trained thinkers available to advise on policy for both kings and prelates. Moreover, these thinkers came from the rich, the poor, and the rising middle class, so the universities significantly advanced social levelling. New ideas were proposed and investigated. They perhaps were not publicly investigated without signals of acceptance from the Church, but universities contributed substantially to the economic and political ferment of the late Middle Ages. They created the role of the disinterested advisor, a role that universities still play today in many societies. The line is a difficult one to walk, but universities do it well, and always have.

Colleges, Halls, Universities

Very early in the development of universities came the linked development of colleges and halls. Where the university received its charter and its principal funding either from a monarch (or a very rich noble) or from the pope or a church prelate, the colleges and halls could be founded and endowed by lesser beings, or even just built up by tenacious and pugnacious masters. The earliest ones were founded by the masters themselves, when they needed housing for their students and room for their own lecturing and teaching. Thus Robert of Sorbonne's foundation of a house at Paris, by gift of the king initially, and eventually his organization of a whole group of houses into an entity that was named for its founder, marks a clear establishment of an entity that is part of the university but not directly answerable in all respects to the rector and his minions. This pattern replicated itself, and indeed was already in place at Oxford and perhaps at other universities as well. An individual master at a university often found the collection of fees rather strenuous, depending as it did both on attendance at his lectures and the pecuniary stability of his scholars; in large part his unenviable job was to collect his fees directly from the students attending his lectures, which meant on occasion a disappointingly low sum of money—after major holidays, or late in the term when students ran short. It was therefore a common pattern for an individual master to supplement his income from lecturing with the provision of a house or houses for scholars, who would pay him both to take care of the necessaries of life for them and for his oversight of their studies. Of course, the same students who ran short of money to pay for lectures did the same for their accommodation and meals, preferring to spend their cash on books or on carousing in the streets. The result was something of a mixture, with some colleges sponsored or owned and run outright by various ecclesiastical orders (notably the mendicant orders including the Franciscans and Dominicans) or by nationalistic groups by planning or chance (at Paris, colleges of Navarre, Denmark, Narbonne, Uppsala) or by masters catering to particular kinds of graduate students (law or theology, notably). The Sorbonne, as discussed above, was the first secular foundation of a college and especially of a graduate college since its entrants were focusing on advanced work in theology. However, the full flowering of the collegiate system was in England, at Oxford and Cambridge principally, but also at the other ancient foundations. Some *hospitia* began as halls for poor scholars, or for scholars from particular geographic areas or backgrounds; others had more random backgrounds (at Leuven, the four houses of the Faculty of Arts were called Lily, Porc, Falcon, and Castle).

The advent of the college and the hall happened differently in different locations. Some cities recognized the real benefit of having a university in their midst, while deploring the natural excesses of the students whose average age was sixteen to eighteen, and provided various incentives. Some citizens would rent rooms or entire floors to students and their entourages. Some of these rooms became designated for specific kinds of visiting students (relatives of the masters, individuals from the same home region as the homeowner) and the costs remained low; others unsurprisingly saw an opportunity for profit, and rents in the major university towns had a tendency to slip upwards. Sometimes laws were passed to prevent this, and sometimes moral suasion was used. Sometimes universities threatened to use their right of *cessatio*, the right of the entire polity to strike (sadly no longer enforced) and not to teach or work as a way of forcing the town to offer redress for an injury. Such injuries usually began in wrangles between students and citizens. The most extreme use of *cessatio* would be to suspend the university's activities completely and move to another town. When other towns, and notably monarchs of other regions, caught wind of a *cessatio*, they sent beguiling letters of invitation to the masters and scholars. Cambridge seems to have started as a result of a partial *cessatio* at Oxford. Henry III of England involved himself in the great *cessatio* at Paris between 1229 and 1231, inviting the university to relocate in his domain, to whatever location they might select and prefer. His offer probably shortened the *cessatio* and contributed to the successful outcome, in which the masters and scholars negotiated yet further privileges.

Housing, then and now, was therefore a major issue. Given the difficulties with rent control (homeowners when balked from charging for the room started to work out ingenious methods of charging for a roof or a door), it is not surprising that handling the issue of accommodation became something the new universities wanted to do themselves. Indeed, universities today run highly profitable housing empires, carefully called "residences" and presented as a favour to the student, allowing the young scholar easy access to the rest of the campus, as well as certainty of quality and continuity of both a bed and subsistence meals (or, nowadays, higher-quality gourmet food). Initially, however, the young arts students were left entirely to fend for themselves, as the first colleges followed the model of the Sorbonne and collected together only the graduate students following the higher degrees. Thus Merton University, Balliol at Oxford, and even the foundation by Edward II of the King's Hall, a location for the education of his household scholars, smacks of this kind of elitist structure. The foundation of New College, propounding a mixed undergraduate and graduate student body, provided the model for what later became common practice in Oxford and Cambridge.

A further issue in the development of colleges and halls is the extent of ecclesiastical influence. Since the masters of the universities in most European cities had established a surprising amount of autonomy, given the general importance of the Church in the twelfth century, it is perhaps not surprising that colleges became a new locus for engagement. The earliest colleges, since they were founded in northern universities of the Paris type, were founded by masters who were members of the clergy, and they found themselves engaging in extensive chantry services for their donors and patrons. Oxford in particular suffered from this difficulty by comparison to Cambridge, which had only three episcopal founders among its thirteen colleges established in this period. As Allan Cobban points out:

Of the ten secular colleges founded at Oxford between the late thirteenth and the end of the fifteenth century, nine had ecclesiastical founders, comprising five bishops, two of Winchester (New College and Magdalen), one of Rochester (Merton), one of Exeter (Exeter), and one of Lincoln (Lincoln); an archbishop of Canterbury (All Souls); an archbishop-elect of Rouen (University); an Oxford rector and chancery clerk, who associated Edward II as co-founder (Oriel); and a chaplain in the house of Queen Philippa (Queen's).[26]

Although the original structures of the colleges varied, by the late medieval period they all involved a group of masters democratically electing the rector (although many terms for the college's leading figure were already in place). Some colleges originally had external procurators, or a veto for the university rector or chancellor, but these disappeared fairly quickly. All of the colleges quite rapidly became vehicles for conservative orthodoxy (especially after the fourteenth-century flirtation with heresy in Oxford involving John Wycliffe and his disciples), and for conservative thinking more generally. The system of colleges and halls, begun as a method of obtaining accommodation for students and funding for masters, and perhaps more charitably as a way of funding poor students in particular, became by the end of the Middle Ages the salient feature of the medieval university.

Many features of the college survive to the present day: extensive endowments for student scholarships and bursaries; endowments, called a loan chest, in aid of the suddenly impoverished fellow, student, or former student;[27] the principle that universities should provide residence services to their students; the requirement of care, which the modern university continues to take very seriously; and the glorious architecture. Most striking, perhaps, is the insular and conservative nature of the college, an entity for teaching and for accommodation.

The Physical and Fiscal University

The medieval college also gave the modern university its characteristic architecture, the Collegiate Gothic mode. Merton College had the first proper quadrangle, though it was established in a somewhat higgledy-piggledy way in the 1260s when Walter de Merton bought and connected up a series of houses, then built a dining hall to go with them. Corpus Christi College Cambridge, founded by the guild of Corpus Christi in Cambridge in response to the Black Death, had the first purpose-built front quadrangle, made quite small because the townspeople of Cambridge could afford no more. The first grand quadrangle in a thoroughly ecclesiastical Gothic style that remains instantly recognizable as a "university" look was the Chapel Quad of New College. The principal reason for the quadrangle system is sometimes lost in consideration of the ways it provides elegance, height, and often green space in the centre. The main reason was that part of the early ethos of the colleges was to have more senior students and masters overseeing the work of more junior students, and the only effective way to do that was to have them in close proximity to each other, in groups of manageable size. The effect of the "staircases," which replicate the original houses that were the first halls of university residence, was to provide an opportunity to mix masters with scholars, and thereby to keep close watch over the high jinks of the undergraduates, and a personal connection to each scholar should discipline or stronger sanctions be needed. The regent masters of each college lived in the college, with the scholars, and could exercise the closest possible supervision of the young men in their care. They were stacked on the staircases above and below them, precisely where inebriation and possible chicanery could most easily be noticed. The chapel and the hall are in line with each other in the New College quadrangle, and the founder's library and large common area for the fellows and masters both have extensive ranges of windows on both sides of the rooms, so that oversight could be maintained (and, as an added benefit, lots of light allowed in for work in the library). New College men, having been trained up at Winchester College, also founded by William of Wykeham, were going to be in good intellectual and physical condition through their studies at the new College of St. Mary of Winchester in Oxford. Excess was discouraged in every way, from the motto ("Manners Makyth Man") to the quadrangle system. From this highly practical and structured physical space emerge the campus landscapes of today.[28]

Paul Temple has recently pointed out that "The great universities of the world are, to a large extent, defined in the public imagination by their physical form: when people think of a university, they usually think of a distinctive place, rather than about, say, the teaching or the research that might go on there."[29] Even the most modern of modern universities builds its physical space either in consonance or in opposition to the deeply ingrained sense of what a university is. And what a university is physically, even today, involves the medieval quadrangle. What began as a system that would integrate scholars and masters, lecture halls and dining halls, chapels and libraries so that a student could and should spend all his time within the hallowed halls of the ecclesiastical-appearing institution in which he had matriculated, is nowadays the model for the integration of lecture halls, faculty offices, small and large classrooms, learning common space, laboratories, and other necessary physical elements of the modern university. Residences nowadays are in some universities interspersed within the quadrangles, and in many circle around the outside, the periphery of the campus, and yet the cloistered sense that a student can spend her university life right on the campus inheres in the mind of every undergraduate and graduate even today.

The quadrangles block out the outside world, and create a real intimacy among students and masters, an opportunity to focus in, to develop, to grow in a safe space. At least, this is the hope. University buildings send powerful messages to their interlocutors, creating their own social capital and a sense of commitment and engagement. They create a kind of "edifice complex" inside the university, fostered by donors (both state and private) who want to stamp their mark on the university. In medieval universities this was an incredibly useful driver of buildings and public spaces, but in the modern era the drive to build—given the growth of virtual and online teaching spaces—may perhaps lessen. Or it may not, for people still really like to see their names on permanent entities like university buildings, classrooms, student common spaces, or even just a carrel in the library.

University finances, even today, are a very murky business. On the face of it, they seem simple: students pay tuition, and after a certain number of years or courses have flowed successfully down the river of gained knowledge, they receive permission to petition for a degree. The university collects the tuition fees paid at matriculation and at set times thereafter, disburses funds to maintain its physical plant and its teaching functions, and whatever remains is turned back into the university system to improve it or to be held for a rainy fiscal day. Yet the situation is never that simple. Universities receive part of their funding, really since the beginning, in grants from governments. Some of these grants are to the capital budget, tagged for the construction of new buildings and given explicitly by monarchs, popes, or various kinds of national, regional, and local governments—and nowadays by titans of industry, incorporated bodies, and serious donors.[30] An amount of the funding goes directly to individual members of the faculty for research or for particular kinds of projects. Some funding comes from individual donors for specific purposes—often benefices for a particular group of students, top-up fund-ing for a particular project, or an endowment to support a particular kind of faculty appointment. The fiscal situation of the modern university is very much a shifting target; and the fiscal situation of the medieval university was very much a shifting target. Many of the early colleges and halls were impoverished, living from month to month and from student fee to student fee or from donation to donation. At the other extreme was the King's Hall at Cambridge, a direct endow-ment that attracted to Cambridge as a whole a great deal of wealth and power (with, unusually, the warden appointed by the king and serving only at the pleasure of the crown, the only such appointment not elected by the fellows or masters). The advent of the king's household at that univer-sity in the mid-fourteenth century transformed its funding model. However, Paris remained the more usual model, with some well-endowed colleges and some barely surviving, and others not surviving. At one point there were nearly seventy colleges at the University of Paris, some of them theological colleges or religious houses, but the majority of them teach-ing institutions for students in the Faculty of Arts.[31] About fifty such entities existed at each of Oxford and Cambridge, later to be amalgamated and absorbed into the larger and fewer houses of the sixteenth and seventeenth centuries. That is, the university system of the Middle Ages involved a shifting mixture of government funding, support from the district or the local bishop, and fees from charging students for matriculation in the university and with the appropriate master, with annual fees for both thereafter, as well as indi-vidual charges for lectures and for other necessities (some universities, nations, or houses also sold books or parchment for profit), especially housing and food. In this respect the medieval university replicates exactly the complex funding model of the modern university. To take but two examples, bookstores today are barely breaking even, and they may be gone in the next generation, whereas in North American universities the practice of funding athletic scholarships (rather than the medieval scholarships for students in particular faculties or from particular nations or towns) continues to grow apace.

Conclusion

Few universities avoid existing within arm's length of a financial crisis; even those that do, because of substantial endowments and emoluments, are likely to have crises in particular elements of their work. Universities, by the nature of their structure, are not particularly good at adaptive leadership, at innovating and learning new competencies. In the business world, this would be the standard response to financial peril: innovation, change, restructuring, challenge. In a university, the standard response is bunkering in and ignoring the problem. This is not at all inexplicable; the resistance to change in a university comes precisely from its longevity as an institution. Hospitals, democratic governments, banks, medium- and large-size businesses, schools as a general enterprise, the entire network of social support systems: all of these postdate the university. This very longevity inoculates the faculty in a given university against the rhetoric of panic, as mostly faculty members know that universities are long-lasting institutions, unlikely to be allowed to collapse. The university structure is a highly resilient one that can withstand a lot of havoc, even a lot of abuse. More particularly, as this chapter has demonstrated, the fundamental structure of the modern university reflects the structure of the universities of Paris, Oxford, and Cambridge, with its wholehearted dependence on the masters, on the teachers, on what today we call the faculty, for the organization and governance of the institution. Since these are the people who understand the basic purpose of the university, to teach and to learn, they are the ones who can most readily discharge the obligation of overseeing its functions. As a result, a modern university that wishes to be respectable and reputable tends to maintain that fundamental structure (or, at least, its appearance). A university may not often need its faculty to flex its muscles and pay close attention to the business of running the university, but it absolutely needs the faculty to have that right and that duty. A university that does not have its faculty at the heart of its governance structure does not have a sufficiently strong structure. It will sway to the winds of change, alter its trajectory from decade to decade, swing to the beat of the current pundit or the current craze, leap to the economic opportunity of the latest fad or enrolment proposal, lose its way among all the competing ideologies, and falter at the hurdles of the modern, the postmodern, and now the posthuman society.

Notes

[20] http://sourcebooks.fordham.edu/source/courcon1.asp (accessed October 1, 2016).

[21] R. W. Southern, *Western Society and the Church in the Middle Ages* (Harmondsworth: Penguin, 1970), p. 279.

[22] Haskins, *The Rise of Universities*, p. 16. Haskins's book is the most elegantly brief treatment of this topic in existence.

[23] The development of Paris is much analysed, and does have some recent scholarship: see C. Stephen Jaeger, *The Envy of Angels: Cathedral Schools and Social Ideals in Medieval Europe, 950–1200* (Philadelphia: University of Pennsylvania Press, 1994), which has a broader remit than Paris but frequently finds itself drawn back there for the quality and quantity of the records available. For Paris only, see Astrik L. Gabriel, *The Paris Studium: Robert of Sorbonne and his Legacy. Selected Studies* (Notre Dame: United States Subcommission for the History of Universities, 1992). Note that Notre Dame hosts the Astrik L. Gabriel Universities Collection at the Medieval Institute Library.

[24] See Pearl Kibre, *The Nations in the Mediaeval Universities* (Cambridge, MA: Mediaeval Academy of America, 1948) for a detailed

study of the characteristics and functions of the nations in Bologna and Paris principally, but also including analysis of other universities in Italy, France, and Spain, and in Northern Europe, including at Aberdeen where the nations survived well into the twentieth century.

[25] I found this story in John Venn, *Early Collegiate Life* (Cambridge: Heffer, 1913), pp. 5–7, part of a speech given by Venn at a Founders' dinner in 1898 in his capacity as President of Gonville and Caius College, Cambridge. The story seems to have happened in 1595, as Neville was only very briefly principal at Brasenose. An irrelevant aside here is that he was also a great fisherman, and has been credited with the invention of bottled beer, so that he could sustain himself while awaiting the first bite on his lures.

[26] See Alan B. Cobban, *The Medieval English Universities: Oxford and Cambridge to c. 1500* (Aldershot: Scolar, 1988), p. 133. On the halls, see also Alfred B. Emden, *An Oxford Hall in Medieval Times: Being the Early History of St. Edmund Hall* (Oxford: Clarendon Press, 1927), and Cobban's *The King's Hall within the University of Cambridge in the Later Middle Ages* (Cambridge: Cambridge University Press, 1969), and the chapter on the "European Collegiate Movement," pp. 122–59 in his *The Medieval Universities: Their Development and Organization* (London: Methuen, 1975).

[27] These were literally chests. At New College, Oxford, the chest was held in the specially built Muniment Tower. Other colleges held theirs in nearby churches or in the bursar's office. See Roger Lovatt, "Two Collegiate Loan Chests," in *Medieval Cambridge: Essays on the Pre-Reformation University*, ed. P. N. R. Zutshi (Woodbridge: Boydell, 1993), pp. 129–65. Pledges included manuscripts, silver vessels (often for ecclesiastical purposes), vestments, and even the odd astrolabe.

[28] For some discussion of medievalizing architecture, see John M. Ganim, *Medievalism and Orientalism* (New York: Palgrave MacMillan, 2008), especially "The Middle Ages as Display," pp. 83–107. On cathedrals as medievalist structures central to their communities, see Elizabeth Emery, *Romancing the Cathedral: Gothic Architecture in Fin-de-Siècle French Culture* (Albany: State University of New York Press, 2001) and *Artistic Integration into Gothic Buildings*, ed. Virginia Chieffo Raguin, Kathryn Brush, and Peter Draper (Toronto: University of Toronto Press, 1995).

[29] Paul Temple, "Frontispiece," to *The Physical University: Contours of Space and Place in Higher Education*, ed. Paul Temple (London: Routledge, 2014). The papers in this volume are excellent and innovative.

[30] An elegant American analysis of the effects of donors on buildings and by extension on the primary function of the university is Kathleen Davis, "Tycoon Medievalism, Corporate Philanthropy, and American Pedagogy," *American Literary History* 22 (2010): 781–800.

[31] See Gabriel Compayre, *Abelard and the Origin and Early History of Universities* (New York: Charles Scribner, 1893), p. 194.

Chapter 3

Curriculum

Today a seventeen-year-old Danish student planning to study physics can decide to start her degree in Belgium at the University of Leuven in order to do some physics in French; in second year, she might check the rankings of the top universities in her field, and although Leuven is in the top one hundred, she might decide to switch to ETH Zurich, the Swiss Federal Institute of Technology, which is in the top ten.[32] Also, she can use that year to perfect her German, which could use some work. For her third year, now that she is comfortable in German, she could move to RWTH Aachen University in northwest Germany. It's closer to home, has an excellent reputation, and she knows that when she takes her final examinations she will attract attention for scholarships in Germany and in the European Union more generally. She is thinking about University College London for graduate school, or perhaps one of the big American universities. Also in her mind is that, during her graduate work, her time in Zurich might be useful to her as an *entrée* to the big European physics project, the Large Hadron Collider built by CERN, the European Organization for Nuclear Research near Geneva. Can such a program be followed today, with a student moving from one university to another in Europe (with perhaps a summer term in Brazil, an internship in Australia, or a work term in Israel, all places with excellent physics programs)? Perhaps not yet, although a globalized education has been a goal in Europe for about thirty years, and the desire to engage in a university experience that will offer this kind of richness and breadth is spreading around the world. Is this entirely a modern experience? Well, no.

In Shakespeare's play, my young Danish student's ancestor Hamlet (indirectly, through a cousin) asks his uncle the king for permission to return to university. In the same play, Laertes heads off for further study at a different university that, judging by the amount of advice he is given by his prolix father Polonius, is going to be a whole new experience for him. Later in the play, Shakespeare uses the training that both have received, at different locations, as something of an excuse for the great plan to have them duel. While they were at university, putatively pursuing the *studium generale*, it is clear that both spent a lot of time on sword play, learning from different fencing masters. Their duel in the last act of the play is a cross-cultural moment, of a sort. For my purposes, it highlights that portability of students and of courses was very much a feature of the late sixteenth and early seventeenth centuries. There was obviously no difficulty with the idea of studying for a while at Wittenberg, returning home for a while, and then returning to the same university or heading onwards to a different institution for a while. (Today, of course, we make something of a fetish of the need to stay in university, to keep at it solidly for three or four years and complete the first degree.) The medieval universities of Europe were fully integrated until late in the fifteenth century, and well into the sixteenth century. They offered extremely similar curricula. A medieval student could spend a year or two at the Sorbonne in Paris, a year at Oxford, a year at Heidelberg, and a year or three finishing off the extra courses for a law qualification at Bologna. Students followed good lecturers, and would travel to hear an Abelard, an Irnerius, an Albericus, a Roger

Bacon. Their mobility meant that, so long as they acquired a master, using letters of reference from the last master, they could take their final examinations in whichever institution seemed best to them. Over the centuries some universities taught principally the *studium generale*, and others taught one or more of the *studia particularia* in addition to the liberal arts curriculum of the *studium generale* or in place of it. Some became highly specialized, or began as highly specialized endeavours: Salerno, for example, was always a medical school, and Bologna fairly early developed a real and very long-lasting interest in law. Its daughter institution (twice, by way of two separate moments of influx from Bologna) of Padua excelled both in the humanistic studies of the *studium generale* and in law, achieving real heights of excellence in the sixteenth century. The portability of the medieval student, and to some extent the portability of the medieval master, was an accepted and standard phenomenon. To the modern eye, this notion of students and masters moving about the world (tempted, for example, to Toulouse from Paris by the offer of better treatment and a stronger program) seems odd. Or does it? Since the Bologna accords of the late twentieth century, initially agreed in 1999 by the education ministers of the countries of Europe, the demand for portability of credits has grown deafening. Many modern universities are steadfastly shutting their ears to this din, but soon they will be unable to prevent a modern *ius ubique discendi* (the right to learn anywhere) corresponding to the relatively unsuccessful charter offered to various masters in the medieval period, the *ius ubique docendi* (the right to teach anywhere). The *ius ubique docendi*, while not particularly successful in the individual medieval university, which tended not to approve of masters just arriving and setting up their own teaching and lecturing without reference to the local dignitaries and university administrators, is the foundation of the principle that master's and doctorate degrees, and to a lesser extent the baccalaureate degree, are universally recognized. A degree is a degree these days. Moreover, a shifting pattern in the modern age closely resembles the medieval period. Degrees in the modern era have steadily more components in them that resemble the medieval approach: study, return home for a while to do something else, study a bit more, study somewhere else for a while, return to the town of your university studies and take one or two courses while working part-time, and only after some years contemplate completing the degree. Nowadays we have different terms for these components: work experience, exchange programs, study abroad, transferable credit, internship, co-curricular learning, and so on. The Bologna accords (strikingly enough agreed at the earliest university, founded in the very late eleventh century) are reversing us back to the medieval notion of varied, portable, and practical learning.

The portability of study in the Middle Ages actually owes itself to practices in the monasteries, nunneries, and cathedral schools of the ninth and tenth centuries. It was common practice for students, once the basic knowledge of the *trivium* had been gained, to travel to a larger local institution for training in the *quadrivium*, and then farther afield for further education. Thus, Charlemagne assembled around himself an international coterie of scholars, tempting Alcuin (from York), Joseph Scottus (from Scotland), Theodulf of Orleans (from Spain), Paul the Deacon (from Lombardy), Paulinus of Aquileia, Peter of Pisa, and many besides. Others came and went as well, so that Charlemagne could foster debate and learning. A second well-known example is Gerbert d'Aurillac, who studied first in the local monastery of Saint-Gerald in Aurillac, but whose obvious excellence and aptitude for science took him to Muslim Spain in the latter half of the tenth century, from which he brought to Rheims and western Europe the astrolabe, the abacus, Arabic numerals, and a grounding in scientific method that allowed him to develop celestial globes, armillary spheres, and a refined version of the astrolabe. His training in Catalonia gave him the groundwork for bringing many technological innovations to France and Italy, although later in life he focused more on politics, rising to an appointment, at the behest of Otto III, as pope Sylvester II. Given that Gerbert seems to have been a peasant, discovered by the abbot of the monastery at Aurillac, mobility for those capable of learning does seem to have been an option before the millennium, and the idea of moving about Europe in order to learn was certainly a feature of the early development of universities. Helen Waddell argues that the first half of the twelfth century was perhaps "the greatest half-century of the Middle Ages," since it had:

> Abelard lecturing in Paris; Peter the Venerable travelling in Spain and commissioning a translation of the Koran; Adelard of Bath in Syria and Cilicia, writing his book on natural philosophy and dedicating it to the Bishop of Syracuse; Hermann of Dalmatia translating the *Planisphere* of Ptolemy and dedicating it to Thierry of Chartres, "the soul of Plato reincarnate, firm anchor in the tempest-tossed flux of our studies"; Thierry lecturing on the new Aristotle, just restored to scholarship: Paris for the first time become the *patria* of the mind, the rival in men's hearts of Rome.[33]

Anyone could discuss anything in Paris in the early twelfth century; arguments could be won and lost on purel intellectual and philosophical grounds, theology worked in harmony with searching out new kinds of knowledge and recovering the ways of thought of Muslim and Jewish scholars for Christian ones to ponder. A halcyon time indeed. It does seem a bit unlikely.

Student portability, the practice of moving from one institution to another, has more restrictions in the modern era than it did in the medieval world, when a student arriving at a new university simply had to find a master willing to take him on as a student and register with the master and the chancellor. Today we have a whole paraphernalia of course equivalencies, and universities prefer that students follow paths that they have laid out: exchanges with specific institutions, or sanctioned moves that involve the continued payment of fees at the home institution. The portability of faculty is similarly circumscribed in the modern day, as a faculty member nowadays moves from one institution to another only with a job offer. That said, portability is on the increase in the modern day, and it may well be that this is a way in which the modern university is coming to resemble the medieval one more by happenstance than design. The basic underlying principles remain the same: to teach and to learn in the most salubrious circumstances.

Studium generale, studium particulare and the Extracurricular Life of a Student

Students began their university lives very young, sometimes as young as thirteen or fourteen, although by the late medieval period fifteen seems to be something of a standard. What the survey of the lectures and learning they had to engage in demonstrates clearly is that they were in lectures for limited hours each week. Even if the lectures on Aristotle's *Ethics* were daily, and it seems unlikely that they were, they were for an hour. Students needed a copy of the Bible, made by themselves, or purchased or hired, and they needed to be aware of commentary on that text, as well as the rest of the set texts in the *studium generale* or in the higher field they were addressing. The lectures were given in sets, and students do not seem to have paid each term for more than two or three sets of lectures (some statutes limited them to three sets of lectures), which basically means that each term they had some preparation work to do on copying their set texts, some time in lectures, and some time studying alone or perhaps in a small group overseen by the regent master of their house. This leaves a great deal of free time, and all the evidence suggests (and on this point the evidence is copious) that they spent that time growing up, getting into as much trouble as possible, eating and drinking to excess, and generally doing precisely what every parent fears a teenage boy is likely to do. The few that were highly studious and likely to continue on for the full course of study to join the masters could certainly swot away if they so desired, but most of the medieval scholars had a rich outside life. Hamlet and Laertes seem to have used at least some of their time honing their fencing abilities, according to Shakespeare. Certainly scions of the nobility, notably elder sons, would need to continue their training in war and strategy. There would still be plenty of time for pursuing personal interests, whether those included gambling, fishing, fighting in the streets, or learning the vernacular language of the country in which one was studying—rather than simply conversing, as the university statutes demanded, at all times in Latin.

Then, as now, students grew up while at university. But the rich and well-to-do students who could afford to pay their fees for years upon end without attending their lectures or contemplating the hard work of studying for their final examinations were by no means the majority. This would vary to some extent from university to university, but a considerable amount of evidence suggests that the greater numbers of medieval students were as poor as Chaucer's famous "clerk," needing various kinds of benefactions and taking time every now and again to earn enough funds to return to their studies. Poorer students while at the university could of course supplement their incomes in various ways: they could become assistants, servants, and even secretaries for the richer ones; they could, for example, earn money copying texts needed for lectures, and the evidence sadly suggests that they could also attend those lectures and take notes for their wealthier counterparts. Part-time work while at university started a long time ago. It should be noted that the majority of students in medieval universities fell into this category. Astrik Gabriel has determined that 64.5 per cent of the students in the Faculty of Arts at the University of Paris were poor or marginal students.[34] Students without any means at the time of matriculation were permitted to list themselves as paupers on the reception rolls. They lived in sometimes quite miserable conditions (the house set aside for poor German scholars in Paris was in particularly dire straits), and worked their way through their studies. Thus, rather than being preponderantly the playground of the rich and powerful, universities were places where the poor but intelligent worked to develop enough knowledge and practical skills to be able to obtain a post. Universities in the Middle Ages were extremely pragmatic institutions.

The *studium generale*, the first program of study, was generally ordained by university statute, and involved a very set group of texts on logic and philosophy. These were the core of the curriculum, including also further study of the *trivium* and the *quadrivium*. Priscian and Donatus were required, since to analyse meaning the young student had to be able to break down the grammar and syntax. Many works of Aristotle addressed issues of logic and science, and Cicero helped students with rhetoric. There were sometimes also lectures on basic issues of grammar and rhetoric, since students needed to hone their writing and argumentation skills. (John of Garland in the thirteenth century prepared a detailed Latin dictionary for his students framed as a descriptive vocabulary walking the young student round the streets of Paris and introducing its food and drink, its workers and streets, its markets and book stalls. He is perhaps an early example of a professor interested in making his material relevant for his students.) Some books on etiquette and good manners also survive, suggesting that, in the early years at university, some basic skills and behaviour patterns needed to be inculcated. In the thirteenth century, the curriculum of the *studium generale* expanded to include many more works by Aristotle now translated from Greek into Latin under the influence of Averroës (Ibn Rushd). It expanded further to include works of natural philosophy (heading in the direction of science) in the next generation. In other words, although the model of set texts implies a certain fixedness of curriculum, in practice the *studium generale* could be quite flexible. Students had to attend lectures, and later in the day the disputations (debates, or perhaps arguments) of their own masters, as well as the cursory lectures given by more senior students in the afternoon. When they had apprehended enough of the curriculum to be able to engage in their own serious work, they embarked on the business of "determination" in which they worked out their own arguments, presented and defended them, and successfully competed for their degree.

The *studia particularia* are something of a separate issue. Medicine was always on one side, a taught program in the way the other curricula were offered, with formal readings and the same system of lectures and disputations. It had few or no practical elements. At some universities, students entered directly for medicine, and did not have to complete the *studium generale* beforehand. At others, they did complete the *studium generale* or sometimes just part of that program. The other degrees offered by the faculties in the *studia particularia* were clearly higher degrees. The highest of these was theology, also in many ways the most perilous. The Church paid little attention to the undergraduates engaged in the *studium generale*, but students of theology had to be watched closely and catechized as necessary to avoid unfortunate thoughts and doctrines creeping into their heads. That said, there were far fewer examinations and investigations of this kind than is usually supposed, so that the Arabic and Spanish thinkers banished from the Paris curriculum in the 1215 statutes were by 1254 a fixed part of the required readings, and the few issues that emerged in the schools were usually resolved by weighty tomes and arguments written by scholars like Thomas Aquinas. There was far more academic freedom, even in the pursuit of theology, than we might conjecture. And the theologians were themselves quite disdainful of law as a subject too plebeian for their notice. Charles Homer Haskins notes that they considered it "lucrative" and as something "which drew students away from pure learning toward the path of ecclesiastical preferment."[35] In the thirteenth century, a well-trained canon lawyer could expect a solid job in the massive administrative structure that was the medieval church, or in the retinue of a king or baron. Moreover, as various statutes indicate, the lectures for canon law began at mid-morning, not at six, which was often before dawn. This was a very solid option for those preferring to sleep in, and for those who wished to earn more in their careers. Civil law, offered principally at Bologna but gradually catching on elsewhere in the later Middle Ages, also offered a solid path to a career, since figuring out fair judicial procedures was something needed in every jurisdiction of every nation. Incidentally, just dying out now is the practice of admitting students to law schools in modern universities after completion of two or three years of a liberal arts degree—the standard medieval practice. The practice is dying out not because students are being admitted earlier to law schools, but because the qualification of a completed undergraduate degree, the *studium generale*, is now standard.

To sum up, all or most students at medieval universities completed the *studium generale*, the curriculum now known as the liberal arts. The higher degrees were in law (both canon law and civil law), theology, and possibly medicine (sometimes treated as a first degree, sometimes as a higher one, as it remains today). Entrance to the high degrees was by completion of the *studium generale* with sufficiently high grades, or by completion of a set part of the *studium generale*. The decisions of the masters on the grading and progression of students was final and irrevocable. The masters also established the curriculum, in concert with various higher powers (the various university statutes suggest that kings sometimes dictated the curriculum, other times it was the decision of the masters in concert with the local archbishop, and sometimes various church legates oversaw elements of the curriculum). Then, as now, the curriculum was in the purview of the state and the university. Students who could not afford to pay their tuition and *domus* (accommodation, food, and ancillary expenses) fees received varying amounts of subsidies and reduced fees, from the university itself and from other sources. The evidence suggests that significant sources of funding were available, and that students who did not have the means might live poorly and might take longer to complete their studies, but they could succeed. In other words, in terms of accessibility and student success, the medieval university was very similar indeed to the modern university.

Despite their reputation in the modern era, the curricula available in the medieval university were highly pragmatic. Hastings Rashdall argues that:

> In a sense the academic discipline of the Middle Ages was too practical. It trained pure intellect, encouraged habits of laborious subtlety, heroic industry, and intense application, while it left uncultivated the imagination, the taste, the sense of beauty—in a word, all the amenities and refinements of the civilized intellect. It taught men to think and to work rather than to enjoy.[36]

On the other hand, this system meant that the structures of governance and law, the structures that gave rise to the solidly based systems of the sixteenth and seventeenth centuries, were established by hard-thinking men who understood the application of logic and rhetoric. Many of them had studied law and had a sense of correct procedure and administration. They also had spent so much time at their institutions of higher education that they had seen constitutional democracy at work in the colleges and universities themselves. They knew how to implement good processes and fair treatment of others, how to argue for their existence, and how to write them into existence.

This element of the medieval university is something of a sad discovery. Far from being a bastion of higher learning and executive thinking, the medieval university was a highly pragmatic place. Students studied law because that gave them a very solid livelihood; they completed the *studium generale* because it gave them a good pragmatic education from which they could pursue law; they studied medicine to become medical professionals; and they studied theology if they wanted preferment in the Church. They did not aspire to think deep thoughts; they aspired to acquire posts with good remuneration and benefits. Some few fell in love with learning and studied to become masters in the university. In other words, their motivations were very like the motivations of students today: fiscal, professional, and only in rare cases intellectual.

Achieving Mastery, and Using It

The medieval curriculum involved a very close relationship between learning and teaching. Once the fifteen- or sixteen-year-old young man had completed the first stages of his studies, he became a kind of teaching-fellow, charged with teaching in order to learn more under the supervision of a more senior teacher. This came after it was certain that the young scholar had sufficient Latin to read, write, and converse in the language, and was fully aware of the basic elements of the *studium generale*. In order so to do he would attend morning lectures on the set texts by faculty members, and, to practise disputation, he would engage in some debates himself, as well as attending other scheduled debates. After four or five years (within a century this shortened to two years), the young scholar would swear to having read the texts and attended the requisite lectures, name the master under whom he had studied, and proceed to a two-part examination (the examiners having been chosen by complex but democratic methods) in which the future bachelor would determine his theses and then defend them orally. Once the successful defence had led in the first place to a feast paid for by the new bachelor, he could either proceed to a *studium particulare* in theology, law, or medicine, or continue on in the Faculty of Arts aiming towards mastery of the field. At this point the learning could well become peripatetic, as the regulations in most universities required the same texts to be lectured upon, but not all universities had masters capable and available to lecture on all subjects. Permission to teach, the licence, was also something the future master needed to work on and to defend before an examining board. Permission to incept into the faculty came with strings attached, usually an agreement to stay and teach for at least two years, and to dispute. Getting to this point commonly took many more years. If those years were spent studying towards the higher degrees in one of the other three faculties, then the highest available degree was a doctorate (of canon law, of divinity, of civil law in some places, and possibly—although patterns varied—of medicine, though that came after far fewer years). In the Faculty of Arts, however, mastery was defined by the defended and disputed master's degree, the granting of the licence to teach, the taking of oaths (not being married, not being a member of a religious order, and on the positive side being willing to keep the peace and work for the university's advantage), and the inception into the ranks of the masters.[37]

The structure of a university degree in the present day is not quite as onerous, but it can be close. Once the printing press arrived, the requirement of oral disputation gradually gave way to written papers circulated privately. This requirement survives today, in most modern universities, only in the written submission and oral debate required for a doctorate. The close supervision by one master in the final stages of the bachelor's degree (the "determination" phase) does not exist in many modern universities, which have moved this requirement also upwards to the level of the doctorate, a degree that was—save for the three given above—largely an invention of the twentieth century. A thirteenth-century student could complete a baccalaureate in about five years, and a doctorate in what was said to be a further three (but was often five or six), which compares well to the modern equivalent. The shift to a sixteen-year stint was a fourteenth-century move, and varied according to the particular university. Perhaps the more onerous requirement, already present in the early thirteenth century, was the age threshold: candidates for the highest degrees often had to be at least thirty-five, which does suggest that it was perfectly acceptable for a scholar to be studying for over half of his life. In order to lecture in the university, albeit in the less-important "cursory" lectures of the afternoon, the young scholar had to be at least twenty years of age, in the 1215 statutes at Paris. Only at the age of twenty, then, was there a legitimate opportunity to make money while actually doing the work that the scholar was at university to do.

The path to mastery was therefore a slow one. One account of the life of a beginning student at the major medieval university of Orleans suggests some of the complexities:

> On arriving at Orleans, the new student had to search out accommodation. He could install himself in the home of a professor or with a bachelor or a *licencié* (a licensed tutor). He could also rent a room or a whole section of a house. We have found mention of a cost of 15–20 pounds per year for accommodation and food during the second half of the fifteenth century and at the beginning of the sixteenth century [...] the purchase of parchment, of paper and of books, especially of manuscripts before the advent of printing, took up a great part of the budget. The cost of manuscripts varied from 10 to 30 pounds for legal materials, juridical works or philosophy [...] one must also count the costs of travel, clothing, feasts, free contributions (for feasts and other events), the extra payments required for professors, and one could very easily add up the costs to 501 pounds.[38]

In short, university was a serious business. The age at which a young male embarked upon the *studium generale* appears to have varied somewhat nationally and individually, but generally it was between thirteen and sixteen. This meant at least four and possibly seven years of expenses. Even if the scholar underwent determination after four years, he still could not lecture (save without special permission, which was occasionally given) for several more. If his plan were to become a theologian, he would have fifteen more years of lectures for the *studium generale*, service as a master in a college, and whatever odd bits of extra work he could cobble together before he could achieve the heights of lecturing on theology. Small wonder that the academic world held little appeal for the vast preponderance of undergraduates. In fact, few baccalaureates, let alone higher degrees, were successfully completed at any given medieval university. Jobs were available after a few years of training, and there was little added value to completing the degree.

Moreover, by the fourteenth century the system was open to abuse. The parameters of that abuse will already be obvious. Impoverished scholars, of whom there were a very significant number, would willingly give more and more lectures, and possibly be quite willing to substitute for masters who did not feel willing to lecture early in the morning. Given that from the twelfth century there was a tradition in every university that a master when appointed rector or proctor immediately had to provide a sum of money with which he and his fellows would repair to a tavern so as to "drink the surplus," it seems possible that some masters engaged in the same bibulosity as their students.[39] They might well not have felt capable of close reading and logical progression in their lectures the next morning, let alone dealing with the difficult questions as they came in the texts. Thus, teaching by the underqualified, lazy masters, and payments for various kinds of deeply dubious practices (paying a poor student to do the determination of a richer student, even paying for the degree itself) appear to be relatively common practices by the later medieval period. The 1215 statute notes that there are one hundred feast days in the year, which severely curtails the number of useful days for teaching and learning, and provides wonderful excuses for more inebriation and for the kind of violent altercations that seem to be a hallmark of the medieval university.

Still, the evidence suggests that the medieval master worked hard. Edward II provided a charter to Oxford in 1315, in which he required the fifteen hundred clerks at the university each to say the psalter.[40] This kind of dispensation, a requirement that the masters should repay a benefactor with prayers and benedictions of their own, was quite common. Moreover, the daily round was relatively onerous. Colleges rose daily at 5:00 a.m., with lectures starting at six (or mass, for those not lecturing), supervising student exercises taking up the morning and the afternoon except for the three hours in which the master was himself lecturing, taking meals twice a day in hall, and after curfew in the evenings enjoying the unlovely job of patrolling the quadrangles ensuring that students were in their rooms and behaving properly. Along the way the master had to prepare his lectures, and probably some sermons and disputations as well. He would talk with visiting masters (especially junior ones, who were encouraged to learn at various universities—part of the process of achieving their mastery), and learn about new ideas and works. He would likely prepare his own copies of new works to save money (masters made great use of the college chest, often depositing one manuscript as surety for acquiring the materials to copy a new and exciting tract), and take a few moments each day for some research and for writing his own works, that being what he had spent his life training to do. Not an easy life, nor a lucrative one. I hesitate here to compare the life of the modern university professor: most will recognize the drudgery but also the joy in both research and teaching.

Conclusion

John Henry Newman argues that:

> a University consists, and has ever consisted, in demand and supply, in wants which it alone can satisfy, and which it does satisfy, in the communication of knowledge, and the relation and bond which exists between the teacher and the taught. Its constituting, animating principle is this moral attraction of one class of persons to another; which is prior in its nature, nay commonly in its history, to any other tie whatever; so that, where this is wanting, a University is alive only in name, and has lost its true essence, whatever be the advantages, whether of position or of affluence, with which the civil power or private benefactors contrive to encircle it.[41]

Teaching is the beating heart of a university for Newman. Without teaching, a university is an adult-level babysitting centre ensuring that teenagers entering upon their years of power engage in risky behaviour that does not too greatly endanger their continued existence, whether physical, emotional, intellectual, or psychological; or it is a well-funded private research and innovation centre. Most larger universities call themselves research institutions and focus their energy on attracting research funding and achieving goals that will impact society, but any threat to their undergraduate teaching recalls them to their base budget issues. Funding for research often does not include infrastructure or overhead, and those elements of the research budget generally come as transfers from the operating budget of the university, occluded perhaps by the fact that operating budgets generally do not distinguish the teaching and research functions of the institution. Universities consider teaching and research indissolubly linked, and in some ways they are, since good teaching drives good research and good research drives good teaching—a genuine virtuous circle. That said, the "true essence" of a university, the feature that keeps it alive and vital, is, as Newman puts it here, "the relation and bond which exists between the teacher and the taught." Newman had his firm views on the curriculum, but he recognized that curricular arguments are less important than this relation and bond at the core of the university, this central purpose and function.

The students at a medieval university were an elite few. They studied a set curriculum offered by a small and high-minded group of scholars, and had close contact with the small group of scholar–administrators who established the intellectual and physical walls that allowed university students and faculty to consider themselves an enlightened and entitled elite. They were not as rich as is commonly supposed, and they certainly took an average of six years to complete their basic degree, considerably longer if they remained at the university to take a higher degree. They excelled in close reading, in oral disputation, in rhetoric and the writing of letters (an exercise that was generally assigned early in their studies was the correct creation of a letter to a parent or benefactor requesting the further disbursement of funds towards the progress of the young scholar), and they were of course fluent in Latin. In most cases they had suffered a good deal of corporal punishment along the way, and in many of the colleges they had suffered privations with respect to their housing and sustenance. They had learned not to throw stones or food in hall (many colleges had specific regulations on this point), so they had achieved a modicum of discipline and duty in their lives. They had learned to take notes in lectures (often at speed, since lecturers, by statute, spoke at the pace of a sermon or disputation), and to meditate or ruminate upon the divine knowledge encapsulated in their texts and notes. Finally, they had learned some style, both in the presentation of their arguments and in the production of the feast to celebrate their accomplishments. With such qualities and accomplishments, they could be safely trusted in government, the practice of law, teaching, business, and the Church. Barring the corporal punishment, the Latin, and perhaps the meditation on the divine, we hope for fairly similar accomplishments today.

Notes

[32] University rankings are a major issue these days; the most trustworthy of an untrustworthy lot seems to be the QS rankings: for the subject-specific rankings on physics and astronomy in 2015 see http://www.topuniversities.com/university-rankings-articles/university-subject-rankings/top-universities-physics-astronomy-2015 (accessed October 2, 2016).

[33] See Helen Waddell, *The Wandering Scholars* (London: Constable, 1927), p. 120.

[34] See Astrik L. Gabriel, "Introduction" to *Liber Receptorum Nationis Anglicanae (Alemanniae) in Universitate Parisiensi ab anno MCCCCXXV ad annum MCCCCXCIV*, ed. Astrik L. Gabriel and Gray C. Boyce (Paris: Didier, 1964), pp. 24–27.

[35] Haskins, *The Rise of Universities*, pp. 36–37.

[36] Rashdall, *Universities of Europe in the Middle Ages*, vol. 3: *English Universities—Student Life*, p. 456.

[37] The length and complexity of the process is well explained in Lowrie J. Daly, *The Medieval University 1200–1400* (New York: Sheed and Ward, 1961), chap. 4, "From Apprentice to Master in Six to Sixteen Years," pp. 122–12.

[38] Hilde de Ridder-Symoens, "La Vie et l'organisation matérielle de l'ancienne Université d'Orléans" [Life and the Financial Infrastructure of the Ancient University at Orleans], in *The Economic and Material Frame of the Mediaeval University*, ed. Astrik L. Gabriel (Notre Dame: International Commission for the History of Universities, 1977), pp. 37–49 at 44. Translation is mine. A great deal of work on the cost of university education in the Middle Ages remains to be done; see also Jacques Verger, "Les Comptes de l'Université d'Avignon, 1430–1512" [Financial Accounts of the University of Avignon], in *The Universities in the Late Middle Ages*, ed. Jozef IJsewijn and Jacques Paquet (Leuven: Leuven University Press, 1978), pp. 190–209.

[39] Rashdall, *Universities of Europe in the Middle Ages*, vol. 1: *Salerno-Bologna-Paris*, p. 416. Note also in vol. 3: *English Universities—Student Life*, pp. 436–37, where Rashdall discusses the custom of drinking not just after the successful examination of a student, but indeed during it. Wine was a requirement for the masters as they dealt with the examinees.

[40] H. E. Salter, *Medieval Oxford* (Oxford: Clarendon Press, 1936), p. 110.

[41] John H. Cardinal Newman, *University Sketches*, ed. Michael Tierney (New York: St. Paul Publications, Alba House, n.d.), pp. 45–46.

Conclusion

Universities have always been a paradox. Publicly perceived, with their own connivance, as separate and self-governed entities, hallowed ground where students test their boundaries and learn how and why to engage with the world, they are at the same time embedded in the world, with their metaphorical snouts poking deep into the public purse, their functions watched over and promoted by an array of governing and funding institutions, philanthropic individuals, and highly engaged corporations. Of no other modern institution can it be said so forcefully that the public is the personal. Alumni think fondly of their time at the university, ossifying it through pastel lenses into the nostalgic glory of their youth, the last stop on their trundle through the halcyon world of childhood and growth towards adulthood, the last call before mortgages and the misery of loans, the daily grind, and lunches in paper bags. Governments take a more curatorial role, sometimes rather proprietary, sometimes not, overseeing the accomplishments of this entity, this behemoth, but without venturing deep into its portals, braving the maw that is the apparent complexity of a university's governance structure. Fearing to awaken the beast that cries out (and occasionally screeches) for university autonomy, they sidle up to the issues of accessibility and accountability, hoping not to nudge the beast too much, hoping not to startle it from its usual somnolence. Parents demand access in strident terms, and applicability in stentorian ones, as their marvellous offspring bring stellar accomplishments in the door, but encounter difficult classroom and examination experiences once inside the hallowed halls of an institution that assesses their progeny differently and challenges their independence and social skills in a plethora of ways. Students find themselves navigating personal, social, and intellectual minefields with only their native wit and common sense to help (and nowadays the odd wellness seminar). The whole paraphernalia of a university education can seem overwhelming, a difficult and uncertain prospect, with little promise of utility in the ordinary and mercantile sense of acquiring a job at the end of the process of attending a university and extracting a degree.

Moreover, universities are sites of conflict. Sometimes that conflict breaks into view, with strikes and procedural motions at gubernatorial bodies and demonstrations. Mostly, it does not. Jaroslav Pelikan describes John Henry Newman's analysis of the current state of the university as a "record of hostility," "a crisis," even "a crisis of confidence."[42] Newman thought otherwise in the nineteenth century, as Pelikan did in the twentieth, and as many commentators do in the twenty-first. And yet, the notion of a university as a calm and peaceful place, an oasis of intellectual and spiritual peace, is always and has always been a chimera. From their inception onwards, universities have rather been sites of conflict, nexus-points for disagreement on their principal purpose and function, locations for opposition between the liberal arts and the professional disciplines, and flashpoints for new kinds of "isms" and their reconciliation into the polity—from racism to sexism to the neoliberal hegemony and onwards.

Nonetheless, and yet paradoxically, universities do not change rapidly in response to a crisis, as I noted very early in this project. At their worst and most exercised, modern universities still do not come close to the upheaval and conflict engaged in by medieval universities. We talk about the rapid change we are facing, and yet we do not engage in rapid change. We talk about the amount of civil unrest and illegal behaviour on university campuses, and universities hire more and more security personnel who interact awkwardly in the local and upper-level security systems in place in the broader society, and yet there are few changes in the way the university actually functions. In Canada, recently, a woman filing a charge of sexual assault against a male student at Brandon University was obliged, as the first order of business, to sign a document stating that she would abide by the conclusions of the university's investigations and that she would not speak of the assault either privately or publicly.[43] This situation is a relic of the benefit of clergy, the autonomy first granted to a university by Frederick II (in his case as an in-your-face insult to the Church, but the idea of university autonomy caught on very quickly indeed). The existence of internal codes of conduct regulating student behaviour in faculties, in terms of academic conduct and especially in terms of non-academic conduct, is a relict of the medieval past. It allows, grants, and perhaps even encourages students to engage in poor or stupid (and sometimes criminal) behaviours with some impunity. On this front, surprisingly enough, change is very slow indeed. In the context of this project, a university bringing to bear its autonomy and fear of bad public engagement first is no surprise. The unwillingness to engage in rapid change, whether through fear, respect, or a recognition that a university is a very large entity and once changed it is changed forever, remains a fundamental hallmark of the university context.

In this regard, I should mention four of the many issues that appear only obliquely in this material. First, women were simply nonexistent in the university context as far as the *studium generale* and most of the *studia particularia* were concerned (there is some evidence that women could be involved in the medical schools). Only by wrenching my argument could I have pretended that Heloise was taught by Abelard as part of his teaching project inside the formal purview of the University of Paris. I forebore mentioning her both because the university's practices were not fully in place at the time of Abelard, so she was not formally refused the opportunity to study simply because the mechanism for that refusal had not developed, and because her opportunity to learn came about through her personal connection to Abelard. The other brilliant medieval women about whom medievalists talk, the playwright Hrotsvitha of Gandersheim and the philosopher, musician, and scientist Hildegard of Bingen, both trained outside the university context, studying the liberal arts in their nunneries. Later significant women, such as the mystics, trained outside the university context, and faced criticism and complaint all their lives for their presumption. Probably women moved through the university world in disguise, as they did in the monastic world, but as yet we have no research on the topic. On the whole, it has been an unpleasant shock to be obliged to use gender-exclusive language throughout the project.

Second, the history of the modern university is often told from a foreshortened historical perspective. Many administrators tell their autobiographical stories from the point of their acceptance as an undergraduate to their retirement after a final stint as president, which means that in the modern era there exists a pretty thorough record from the last fifty or so years.[44] Other analyses focus on specific national stories, largely of the present day and providing historical information only to contextualize the story of current approaches in law, medicine, science, and other faculties. Those that provide more context tend to begin at the second world war, and very few offer an approach that engages with the national foundations of a given university system.[45] Underlying most modern assessment of the university system, however, is a dependence on the radical transformation of the institution that began with the work of Wilhelm von Humboldt in Germany. This argument posits that Humboldt conceived the notion of universities as a means of economic production, an engine for social change, and a place of liberal enlightenment. The development of the specialized university, the research university in particular with its focus on the genius professor, dates to this shift towards the practical use of universities in service to society. I have not engaged this argument directly, partly because to do so would have strayed too far from my remit here, but also because I have attempted to demonstrate, at least to some extent, that universities have always been an engine of economic development, and an engine very much in the service of the state.[46] Whether they are committed to social development and to the life of the mind may depend more on the individual university's ethos and financial security rather than on their development as an Humboldtian institution. That is, I believe that despite the cognitive change brought in during the nineteenth century, which caused the perception of the institution to shift somewhat, the basic elements of the modern university are medieval in inception and development, and to a large extent medievalizing in their further development.

Third, some will think deeply naive my construction of the university as a place of masters and students, and will consider foolish my belief that the faculty remain the core of the modern university. They are the group likely to subscribe to the belief that universities are transforming today, that they are serving the higher purpose of society by changing rapidly into much more practical and pragmatic pedagogic locations, with a cleaner sense of their obligation to provide useful support for industry and for innovation.[47] They will also consider ridiculous my faith in tradition, and my belief that universities can and should change slowly and carefully, my simple belief that the transformation going on in the university system at the moment is a transformation best managed by the individuals doing the teaching and the research. For this reason, I have not spoken a great deal about leadership or about the rise of bureaucracy in the university system, not because these are not important issues, but because they are so frequently the only issues discussed and the only changes advocated.[48] It is certainly the case that too many universities are abdicating their genuine responsibilities and handing over all decision-making to well-meaning and intelligent managers and disconnected senior administrators. The disconnect between what is actually happening in the classrooms and research facilities, and what is happening in the boardrooms of the university seems ever greater. And that should not be.

My fourth and last point largely set aside is a different aspect of the benefit of clergy. Where this benefit accrues to students in terms of disciplinary codes and a somewhat lax understanding that they should be responsible for themselves but should be rescued if at all possible—from this understanding grow many policies according university students many special options of care and consideration in terms of health and wellness—the same benefit also accrues to the faculty. Students and administrators understand their roles very clearly and know how to advance their concerns both publicly and privately. Faculty members are far less adept. Tenure, a *de facto* job security enjoyed by very few job classifications in the modern day, is a privilege also deriving from the medieval certainty of post once a master joined a college or university.[49] Globally, tenure is now reserved for the reduced number of faculty members hired by extensive formal processes granting them tenure-track and thereafter tenured status, and the tenure system ignores or avoids thinking about contract academic faculty, hired piecemeal by the course. By its nature tenure does not lead to a lack of research productivity or a stultification in the classroom, but in practice it can, partly because many faculty members do not value their tenure save as job security. In medieval colleges, fellows were appointed for life so that they could get on with doing the work of teaching, worshipping, and running the college. They had no choice but to get along with one another, on the analogy of the monastery or nunnery, so they did so in order to advance the interests of the institution. Modern faculty have the option of doing the same, using their tenure as a muscle that has to be flexed; often, rather like their medieval forebears, they buckle under outside pressures and fear, accepting donations they should not or failing to pay attention to new policies and practices.

The medieval university was a fascinating entity. Originally growing organically out of the cathedral and monastic schools system, by the end of the twelfth century the three or four earliest universities were already establishing strong, autonomous, and highly democratic systems of governance. Even given the two very different structures that began the medieval university, one a system of students organizing and hiring their teachers and the other a system of masters organizing and charging their students, these universities strikingly established strong connections with monarchies and with local officials, and maintained constantly shifting and careful alliances with the Church. In the second and third generations of establishing universities, cities and towns recognized their utility for economic and social advancement, and attempted to establish new universities or recruit members (or indeed entire universities) from existing ones. A system was perforce established of utilitarian buildings for the business of the university administration, but elegant and enduring buildings beautifully spaced around quadrangles for the business of teaching, learning, and living. Young scholars had remarkable careers in the university system, essentially being professional students for the better part of two decades, learning a curriculum that in its essentials was very similar in all medieval universities, but which for the higher degrees had elements of real specialization at particular institutions. The structures of discipline, paying fees and charges, arriving at and graduating from a university: all these elements of the university experience drew upon the liturgy and pomp of the Church, but established fully separate rites and processes. All of these elements of the medieval university exist in the modern university, changed and altered through the centuries, sometimes lost and recreated, sometimes thought to have been developed anew.

Notes

[42] Pelikan, *The Idea of the University*, p. 11.

[43] See http://www.cbc.ca/news/canada/manitoba/brandon-university-behavioural-contract-1.3520568 (accessed October 2, 2016).

[44] My current favourite in this genre is William M. Chace, *100 Semesters: My Adventures as Student, Professor, and University President, and What I Learned Along the Way* (Princeton: Princeton University Press, 2006), but there are multifarious others.

[45] One useful analysis in this respect is John R. Thelin, *A History of American Higher Education* (Baltimore: Johns Hopkins University Press, 2004); see also the papers in *Organization and Governance in Higher Education*, ed. M. Christopher Brown II, 5th ed. (Boston: Pearson, 2000), for a very broadly based set. Many other collections of papers are nation-specific, but focus on the present and the proposed future, and rarely consider the past and the origin stories. As a number of universities have recently discovered, origin stories make a difference.

[46] Those who like numbers and tables will also notice a significant lack here, as I am more interested in ideas and issues. However, an excellent recent book with lots of such information, and with a genuine historical sense even though its focus is wholly modern, is

Robert Lacroix and Louis Maheu, *Leading Research Universities in a Competitive World*, trans. Paul Klassen (Montreal: McGill-Queen's University Press, 2015). It has chapters on the university system in the United States, the United Kingdom, Canada, and France, as well as chapters that consider the global context of the modern university.

[47] On the efficacies of the proposed transformation in university culture and structure, see Harold T. Shapiro, *A Larger Sense of Purpose: Higher Education and Society* (Princeton: Princeton University Press, 2005); Kevin Carey, *The End of College: Creating the Future of Learning and the University of Everywhere* (New York: Riverhead, 2015); and Derek Bok, *Universities in the Marketplace: The Commercialization of Higher Education* (Princeton: Princeton University Press, 2000). All three books take a very American-centric approach.

[48] The debate is more than a bit polemical on one side. See Mary Burgan, *What Ever Happened to the Faculty? Drift and Decision in Higher Education* (Baltimore: Johns Hopkins University Press, 2006) and Frank Donoghue, *The Last Professors: The Corporate University and the Fate of the Humanities* (New York: Fordham University Press, 2008).

[49] A useful survey on the subject is Donald C. Savage, *Academic Tenure and its Functional Equivalent in Post Secondary Education*, Working Paper No. 218 (Geneva: International Labour Office, 2005). Revoked by Margaret Thatcher's government for new faculty in 1988, existing in a somewhat murky void in Australia, tenure remains in most North American and European institutions as the right to continue in post save in conditions of real financial exigency. University faculty associations that have unionized to create a genuine medieval *universitas*, a guild, depend upon both tenure and their certification for seniority and job security.

Further Reading

The suggestions below include some of the more significant works on the history of universities and the modern study of the university, but I have also included some lighter fare, and some lesser-known works that deserve greater fame.

Angus, Ian. *Love the Questions: University Education and Enlightenment*. Winnipeg: Arbeiter Ring, 2009.

Bok, Derek. *Higher Education in America*. Rev. ed. Princeton: Princeton University Press, 2013.

Clark, William. *Academic Charisma and the Origins of the Research University*. Chicago: University of Chicago Press, 2007.

Cobban, Alan B. *The Medieval English Universities: Oxford and Cambridge to c. 1500*. Aldershot: Scolar, 1988.

——. *The Medieval Universities: Their Development and Organization*. London: Methuen, 1975.

Gabriel, Astrik L. *Garlandia: Studies in the History of the Mediaeval University*. Notre Dame: Medieval Institute, 1969.

Haskins, Charles Homer. *The Rise of Universities*. Ithaca: Cornell University Press, 1957.

A History of the University in Europe. Edited by Walter Rüegg. Vol. 1: *Universities in the Middle Ages*, ed. Hilde de Ridder-Symoens. Cambridge: Cambridge University Press, 1992; vol. 2: *Universities in Early Modern Europe*, ed. Hilde de Ridder-Symoens. Cambridge: Cambridge University Press, 1996; vol. 3: *Universities in the Nineteenth and Early Twentieth Centuries*, ed. Walter Rüegg. Online publication. Cambridge: Cambridge University Press, 2007; vol. 4: forthcoming.

Lacroix, Robert and Louis Maheu, *Leading Research Universities in a Competitive World*. Montreal: McGill-Queen's, 2015.

Newman, John H. (Cardinal). *University Sketches*. Edited by Michael Tierney. New York: Alba House, n.d.

Organization and Governance in Higher Education. Edited by M. Christopher Brown, II. 5th ed. ASHE (Association for the Study of Higher Education) Reader Series. Boston: Pearson, 2000.

Rashdall, Hastings. *The Universities of Europe in the Middle Ages*. New ed. in 3 vols. Edited by F. M. Powicke and A. B. Emden. Vol. 1: *Salerno, Bologna, Paris*; vol. 2: *Italy-Spain-France-Germany-Scotland etc.*; vol. 3: *English Universities—Student Life*. Oxford: Clarendon Press, 1936.

Rhode, Deborah L. *In Pursuit of Knowledge: Scholars, Status, and Academic Culture*. Stanford: Stanford University Press, 2006.

Riché, Pierre. *Écoles et enseignement dans le Haut Moyen Age: Les écoles et l'enseignment dans l'Occident chrétien de la fin du Ve siècle au milieu du XIe siècle*. Paris: Aubier Montaigne, 1979.

Schachner, Nathan. *The Mediaeval Universities*. London: George Allen & Unwin, 1938.

Shapiro, Harold T. *A Larger Sense of Purpose: Higher Education and Society*. Princeton: Princeton University Press, 2005.

Les Transformations des universités du XIIIe au XXIe siècle. Edited by Yves Gingras and Roy Lyse. Quebec: Presses de l'Université du Québec, 2014.